A Corpus of Pagan Anglo-Saxon Spear-Types

M. J. Swanton

British Archaeological Reports 7
1974

British Archaeological Reports
122 Banbury Road, Oxford OX2 7BP, England

General Editors:

    A.R. Hands, B.Sc., M.A., D. Phil.

    Mrs Y.M. Hands

    D.R. Walker, B.A.

Advisory Editors:

    C.B. Burgess, M.A.

    Neil Cossons, M.A., F.S.A., F.M.A.

    Professor B.W. Cunliffe, M.A., Ph.D., F.S.A.

    Sonia Chadwick Hawkes, B.A., M.A., F.S.A.

    Professor G.D.B. Jones, M.A., D. Phil., F.S.A.

    Frances Lynch, M.A., F.S.A.

    P.A. Mellars, M.A., Ph.D.

    P.A. Rahtz, M.A., F.S.A.

B.A.R. 7, 1974: "A Corpus of Pagan Anglo-Saxon Spear-Types"

© M.J. Swanton, 1974

The author's moral rights under the 1988 UK Copyright, Designs and Patents Act are hereby expressly asserted.

All rights reserved. No part of this work may be copied, reproduced, stored, sold, distributed, scanned, saved in any form of digital format or transmitted in any form digitally, without the written permission of the Publisher.

ISBN 9780904531046 paperback
ISBN 9781407323527 e-book
DOI https://doi.org/10.30861/9780904531046
A catalogue record for this book is available from the British Library
This book is available at www.barpublishing.com

A CORPUS OF
PAGAN
ANGLO-SAXON
SPEAR-TYPES

CONTENTS

List of Illustrations

Acknowledgements

I	INTRODUCTION	1
	1 Derivative Forms: Series A and B	5
	2 Leaf-shaped Blades: Series C and D	8
	3 Angular Blades: Series E to H	13
	4 Corrugated Blades: Series I to L	20
II	THE CORPUS	25

LIST OF ILLUSTRATIONS

Fig. 1. a Carvoran, Northumberland; b Abingdon I, Berks., grave 69; c Kingston, Kent, grave 173; d Guildown, Surrey, grave 56.

Fig. 2. a Fairford, Glos., Ashmolean Museum 1851 142; b Winchester I, Hants.; c Melbourn, Cambs., grave 12; Harnham Hill, Wilts., grave 17.

Fig. 3. a Polhill, Kent, grave 84; b Linton Heath, Cambs., grave 89; c Prittlewell, Essex, grave 2; d Little Wilbraham, Cambs., Cambridge University Museum 48 1639.

Fig. 4. a Droxford, Hants., British Museum 1902 7-22 109; b Woodbridge, Wilts.; c Barham, Kent, Liverpool Museum 6298; d Wrotham II, Kent.

Fig. 5. a Stratford, War., grave 17; b Sibertswold, Kent, grave 23; c Brentford, Middlesex, London Museum O.2085; d Gilton, Kent, grave A.

Fig. 6. a Folkestone III, Kent, grave 5; b Burford, Oxon.; c Salisbury, Wilts.; d Sarre, Kent, grave 39.

Fig. 7. a Battersea, London Museum A7347; b Droxford, Hants., British Museum 1902 7-22 90; c Brentford, Middlesex, London Museum O.2062; d Harnham Hill, Wilts., grave 14.

Fig. 8. a Fairford, Glos., grave 28; b Barnes, Surrey, Gunnersbury Museum O.2061; c Merrow, Surrey.

ACKNOWLEDGEMENTS

The initial work entailed in assembling this corpus was begun with the aid of a Durham Colleges research grant; it originally formed part of the index to a thesis presented at the University of Durham in 1966.

I should like to record my sincere thanks to the very many individuals and organizations who so generously assisted me in its compilation. Many museum curators have allowed me free access both to their collections and their time, answering all my questions with the utmost patience. And field-workers have spared time to discuss with me the results of their recent excavations. Of major finds as yet unpublished or deposited in museums, I am indebted to Mrs S. C. Hawkes for information on Finglesham and Worthy Park, Mr A. C. Hogarth on St Peters, Mrs M. U. Jones on Mucking and Mr G. Taylor on Welbeck Hill.

Exeter, 1974.   M.J. Swanton.

I   INTRODUCTION

Spearheads are among the commonest of finds from pagan Anglo-Saxon cemeteries and among the most familiar of objects in our museum collections. The characteristic weapon of the ordinary Anglo-Saxon warrior, the spearhead occurs equally in princely graves. Found in large numbers over the entire area of settlement and at every period, the majority of spearheads, like pottery, will have been locally produced and therefore represent a potentially useful cultural index.

Long unregarded, the fact that Anglo-Saxon spearheads have been subject to no systematic study may have been partly due to their unprepossessingly corroded condition, as well as to their very plethora and the inherent difficulties of applying typological definitions to so large and amorphous a body of material. The classification outlined here was based on the compilation of a corpus of Anglo-Saxon spears containing something between three and four thousand entries ascribable to the 'pagan' period. This was compiled from all published references where details other than that of mere incidence are given, and a supplementary assemblage of almost three thousand measured drawings of material made available to me from public and private collections. While important in illustrating such matters as weapon-groupings or funerary customs, however, the scope of the corpus here presented has had to be confined to an index of little more than two thousand entries recording formally classifiable material. Corrosion of iron is considerably accelerated as the object is unearthed, and only relatively recently has immediate remedial action been generally feasible. The slightest of formal features will often survive mere corrosion. But poor treatment in storage or, worse still, over-drastic conservation, has meant that many examples are no longer useful. Even since the initial survey for the corpus was carried out in 1961-2 much evidence has ceased to be available. A recent check suggests that the corpus now represents the only accurate record of many objects now completely unrecognisable or no longer in existence.

In order that it may be readily usable, the system of classification outlined here is essentially formal, based on simple visual characteristics. The major criteria are those of profile and proportion, together with some consideration of cross-section and overall length, and less apparent features such as bulk and weight. Apparently irrelevant features, so far as formal classification is concerned, include such arbitrary socket modifications as the addition of languets, binding-rings, the character or even presence of socket-cleft, and so forth. But while not significant in general, such minor features sometimes contribute to the assessment of a particular class. For instance, the fact that such unusual socket modifications as languets, tanged hafting and so forth occur relatively frequently in the stepped-section series K and L helps confirm their early 'experimental' character. And the fact that these types are commonly inlaid suggests that they were not, as was previously thought, intended for use as missiles rather than hand-spears. Insular-style inlays represent a further link between the formally related series L and H, while inlays of early continental type are confined to two clearly imported examples of group B2. Similarly, the presence of welded sockets in several spearheads of the insular-developed fullered series I assists in identifying its early origin although examples datable by association are rare. Welded sockets are characteristic of only a limited number of early Anglo-Saxon spear-types, all immediately deriving from pre-migration continental forms. Some such examples will have been imported in the hands of their owners, and all may have been the work of immigrant smiths. Welded sockets are sometimes found in small blades with traditional profiles from early contexts, but never in any of the newer angular types that are by far the commonest and most characteristic of Anglo-Saxon forms. By the middle of the sixth century Anglo-Saxon smiths seem universally to have adopted the cleft mode, which became an essentially Anglo-Saxon feature, retained long after its general abandonment in continental forges some time before 600.

Formal as well as technical discontinuity marks the break between pre- and post-migration types. With the exception of just one or two groups, numerically very small, it is difficult to trace any certain history of forms extending over the migration age. With the abandonment of their continental homelands, the relatively simple pattern of forms traditional there seems totally to disintegrate; and by the end of the fifth century traditional types were all but forgotten, surviving if at all only in very modified forms. That insular Anglo-Saxon spearheads should then have assumed such a wide variety, is perhaps hardly surprising. It is now common ground that the initial settlement was effected not by large folk-groups coherent enough to transmit common cultural traditions, but by small and mongrel war-bands whose ultimate origins may have been very diverse. And although broad similarities may emerge, clearly demonstrable links with continental developments are rare subsequent to the settlement proper.

The typological classification of this kind of material is fraught with problems. Any simplistic assumption that there may be 'kinds', rather than simply groups of objects which share common characteristics, proves quite unrealistic in this instance. Unlike the jeweller's castings, each forging is an act of production essentially unique. I have attempted to avoid over-rigid verbal definition, which accommodates neither the decentralised character of production nor its amorphous consequences, and have suggested an elastic sequence of series and groups which might acknowledge more sophisticated formal interrelationships. The identification of a series of overlapping groups, while simply reflecting physical reality, usefully recognises the fact of overlapping or related cultures, geographically or chronologically distinct, and is of value in estimating relative chronologies. Despite even this very broad scheme of classification, however, by no means all examples can be assigned easily to one particular group or another. Some exhibit characteristics of two or more; others seem to lie outside any specific grouping.

Like the axe, the spearhead is a utilitarian form; it alters little, and then due to an occasional shift in function rather than to rapid change in fashion. And this, together with the fact that no widely-dated range of spears exists from any one site, renders any relative chronology based on formal development extremely difficult. While one or two Germanic spearheads come from late Roman contexts in this country, virtually the entire body of material takes the form of grave deposits or unassociated surface- or river-finds. The chronology of pagan Anglo-Saxon archaeology still largely depends on that already established for female ornaments. But while closely datable associations occur only rarely in warrior graves, almost every group includes a number of examples associated with glass, pottery, one of the datable objects like brooches, normally found only in female burials, or one of the small but slowly increasing number of datable male associations - still largely seventh-century attributes - like broad seaxes or sugar-loaf shield-bosses. Where the numerical decay of a group can be observed to have begun during the period for which we have adequate evidence, it may reasonably be assumed that the latest datable examples were in fact among the last of that type in use. But where a group, numerically in favour during the seventh century, is then cut off from archaeological view, it is probable that their manufacture and use continued for some time subsequent to the last ones being buried. There is no strong evidence to suggest that the abandonment of traditional pagan modes of burial coincided with any significant change in military conditions which might have affected weapon-design. On the other hand, such types as we may claim for 'later Anglo-Saxon' are for the most part markedly distinct from those current during the seventh century. The strong, lengthy blades which predominate in late Anglo-Saxon times, their sockets often reinforced by bolstering or lugs and once more commonly welded, seem to imply a mode of use no longer designed to receive the greatest impact at the tip, but one in which lateral and parrying blows are at least equally important.

For a detailed examination of typological, chronological and other considerations, see the author's *The Spearheads of the Anglo-Saxon Settlements* (Royal Archaeological Institute, London, 1973).

DERIVATIVE FORMS

The initial phase of Anglo-Saxon settlement, during which various Germanic groups seem first to have been introduced into Britain, some in the service of the Roman army, others by way of controlled civilian settlement under Roman or sub-Roman patronage, is marked by a limited number of traditional pre-migration spear-types. Some such examples occur in late Roman contexts, others in the earliest Anglo-Saxon graves. Their distribution is sparse but scattered, and compares with that of certain classes of 'Romano-Saxon' material.

Series A comprises the small number of Anglo-Saxon spearheads with barbs. From the third century barbed darts had regularly featured in the weapon-sets buried in north Germanic warrior-graves. And, reduced to just two well-defined types, they represent one half of the finds from the great Danish bog-deposits on the eve of the migration age. **A1** Some plainly derivative pieces come from the hinterland of Hadrian's Wall, the best preserved measuring 55 cms overall: a narrow, flat blade, lentoid in section with broad cut-out barbs on a lengthy solid shank and welded socket (Fig. 1a). No doubt these were introduced by some of those German units whom we know by name to have been stationed along the Wall during the later third and fourth centuries. Others, however, rather shorter, and some of which at least have cleft sockets, come from what were plainly Anglo-Saxon contexts, widely dispersed in the south of England. Chronological evidence is slight but probably in England, as in Scandinavia, this type did not survive the fifth century. **A2** On the continent of Europe during the course of the fifth century, however, there developed a considerable lengthening of a second pre-migration type. The heads of these are long and quadrangular in section, with a strickening in front of long and delicate barbs; or sometimes the head is shorter and more pyramidal in form. But often more than a metre in length overall, the greater part is made up of a slender solid shank on a short cleft socket occasionally reinforced with one or more binding-rings. While found distributed widely throughout Germanic Europe, this type of spear is characteristically the weapon of the Franks, apparently called by them ἄγγωνες. There is some evidence that insular examples covered very much the same chronological range as their Frankish counterparts. But the most securely datable English finds all belong to the seventh century, associated with low-cone shield-bosses and objects decorated in Style II. Several occur in association with Frankish-style objects. And the geographical distribution of this type of barbed dart, like that of other long-shanked types for which convincing Frankish parallels may be adduced, is centred on Kent and the line of the Thames. This type of barbed dart seems not to have survived the middle of the seventh century either in England or on the continent.

Series B comprises two small groups traditional to the Germanic Iron Age. Although formally related only in their remoter pre-migration antecedents, they share in common a mode of construction in which midribbing is the dominant structural feature, placing emphasis on the tip rather than the lower blade when in use. **Type B1** consists simply of the midrib itself: stout, square-sectioned socketed spikes, varying for the most part between about 18 and 30 cms, although some may have been much longer. A few have welded sockets; others are provided only with narrow parallel-sided slits - the prior stage to butt-welding. Despite its relative rarity, there is reason to believe that in England this type spanned the entire pagan period. As in northern Gaul, no doubt the earliest were carried by Germanic comitatenses. And in Kent at least, associated examples occur as late as the seventh century. A Dark Age Celtic version, characteristically triangular rather than quadrangular in section, is possibly identifiable with the *gwyngalch a pedryollt bennawr* of *Y Gododin*. **B2** Another clearly derivative group consists of compositely-welded and midribbed leaf-shaped blades which had survived from earliest La Tène times, albeit now mostly with only light and subdued midribbing compared with their continental antecedents. Some have the wider part of the blade at the bottom with a strickening above (Fig. 1d); others are more regularly foliiform. Sizes vary, but the largest is only 41 cms long. Sockets are characteristically welded, but some are simply hammered close or have narrow slits in otherwise tubular sockets. As a whole, this group seems to belong to the earliest stage of the settlements.

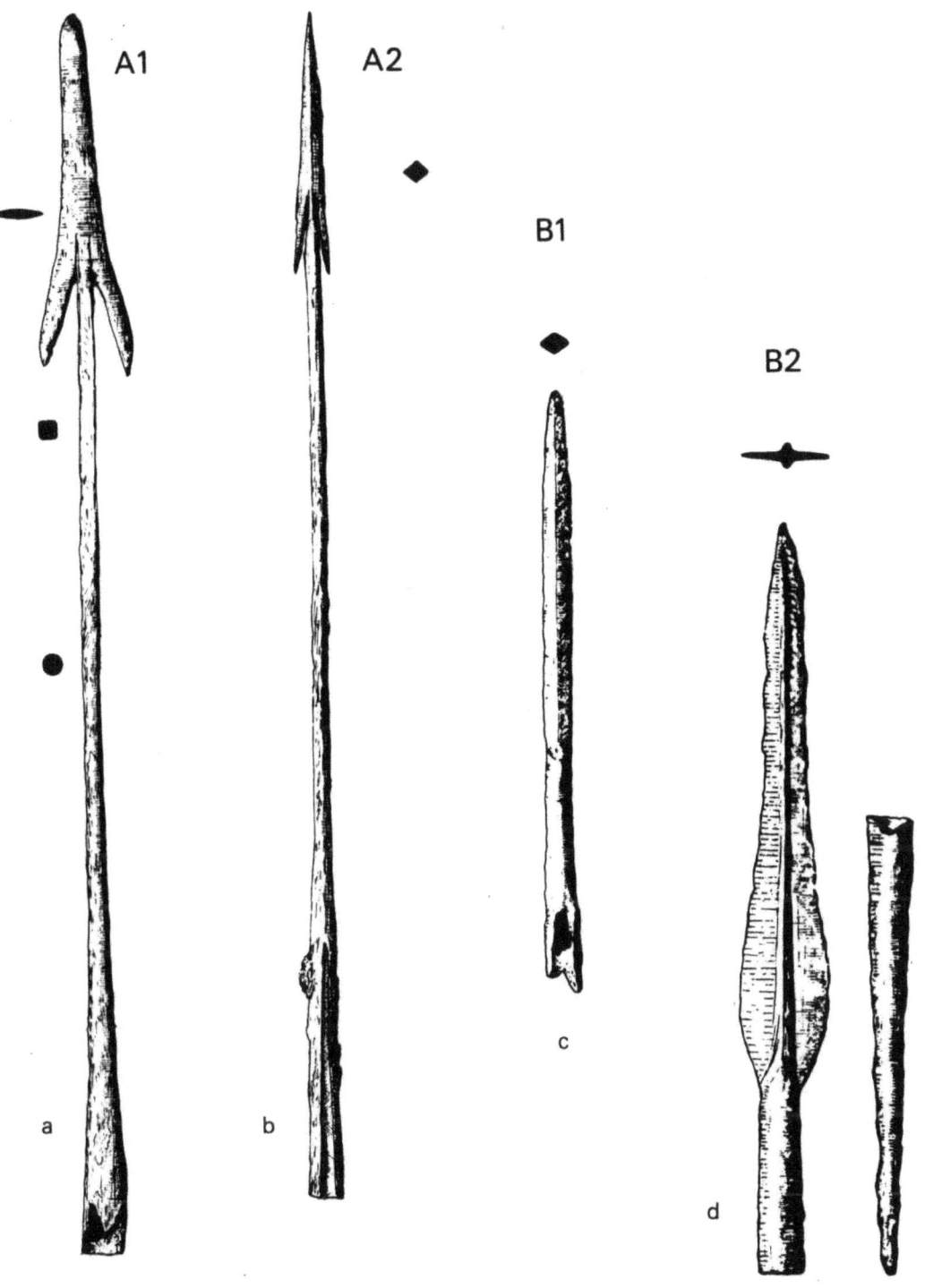

Fig. 1. a Carvoran, Northumberland; b Abingdon I, Berks., grave 69; c Kingston, Kent, grave 173; d Guildown, Surrey, grave 56. Scale ⅓

They occur together with accoutrements of the kind associated with Teutonic auxiliary troops in the upper occupation-levels of late Roman forts, and in Romano-Saxon warrior-graves. Others in patently Anglo-Saxon burials are found in association with late Roman objects. A few pieces richly inlaid in an East Germanic style probably represent direct imports; and all might represent the work of immigrant smiths working in the continental manner. There is no evidence to suggest that this type of spearhead survived the period of initial settlement. By the beginning of the sixth century certainly, midribbing seems to have been replaced by cheaper corrugated substitutes in the insular-developed series I and K.

LEAF-SHAPED BLADES

Series C and D represent the two divergent insular developments from the ubiquitous simple foliiform spearhead of pre-migration times. Unlike angular forms, leaf-shaped blades offer no readily determined point at their edge, and are thus much more difficult to define; and gradations of curvature are not easily classified when disfigured by corrosion. But blade profile is less significant in this instance than overall proportions between blade and socket. Series C is characterised by an increasing proportion of blade to socket, and series D by an increasing proportion of socket and shank length.

C1 Small leaf-shaped blades of the simplest kind, measuring between 10 and 20 cms long, are found relatively commonly over almost the entire area of settlement. As with all leaf-shaped forms, the blades tend to be lentoid in cross-section. A few have sockets still welded; some others, however, have their sockets merely burred over at the upper end - and were perhaps originally bound to the shaft with cord. For the most part these come from only poorly-furnished graves, and few are datable. But associations with late Roman objects and early Anglo-Saxon objects generally suggest an early date-range for this type of spear. Like the smallest of angular blades, this type probably fell out of favour towards the middle of the sixth century when settled conditions made plentiful supplies of raw material, and larger forms therefore, generally more practical. Few were

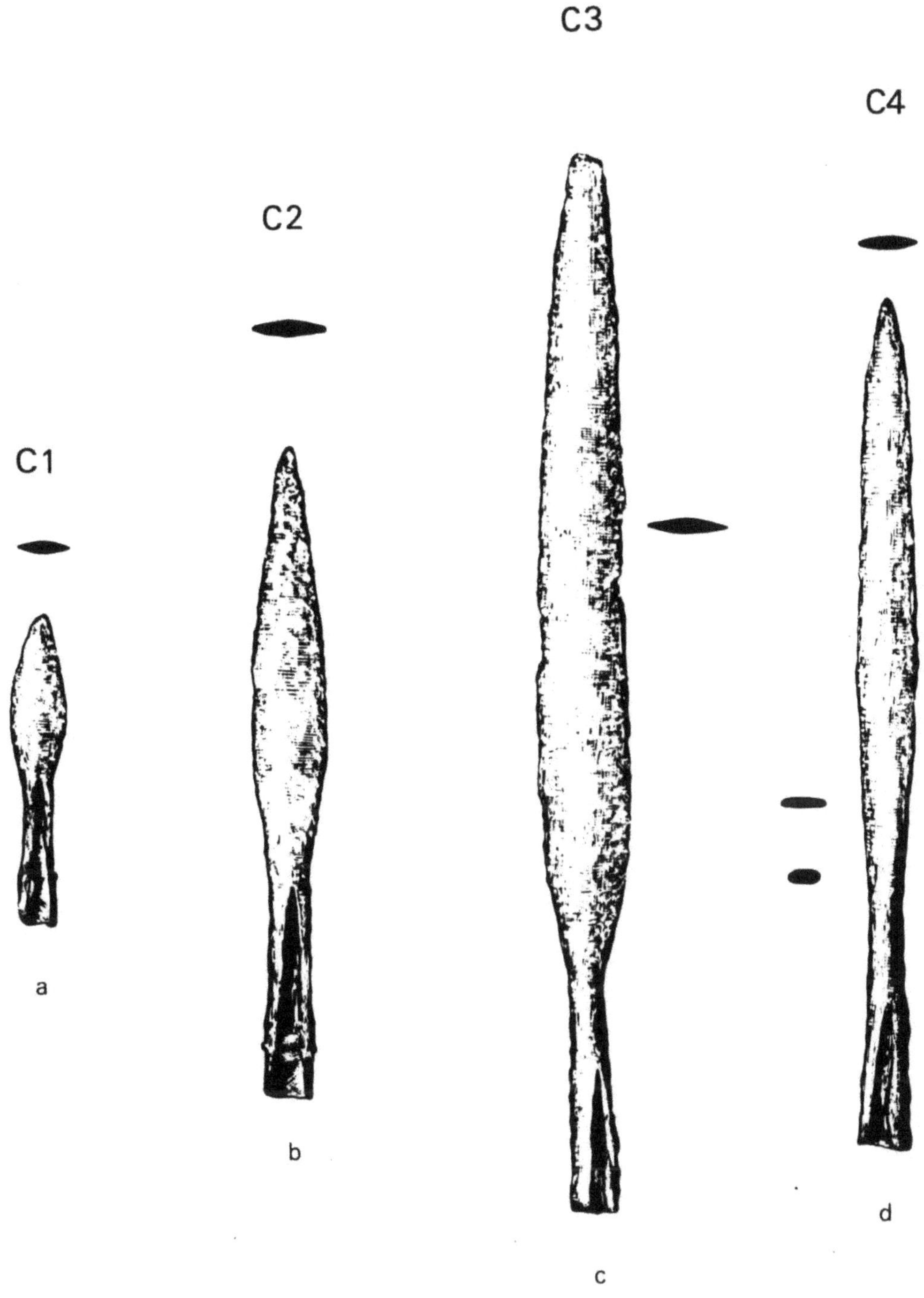

Fig. 2. a Fairford, Glos., Ashmolean Museum 1851 142; b Winchester I, Hants.; c Melbourn, Cambs., grave 12; d Harnham Hill, Wilts., grave 17. Scale ⅓

ever found in the iron-rich kingdoms of Kent and Sussex. And in common with other leaf-shaped forms, they occur only rarely in East Anglia.

C_2 By far the commonest leaf-shaped blades found in Anglo-Saxon graves are much more slender overall than those of the previous type, with a distinctly longer length of blade and a proportionate lengthening of the whole, varying for the most part between 20 and 35 cms. A short solid neck invariably separates the blade from a broadly-cleft socket. Spearheads with this profile are found with associations indicating the widest possible range in time from the earliest settlements to the end of the seventh century. Some with welded sockets come from *limitanei* contexts and from early Saxon graves. But there is abundant evidence to indicate a clearly seventh-century date for many others, found with low-cone shield-bosses and broad seaxes. Indeed, spearheads of this type seem often to accompany the more elaborate seventh-century burials. And continuing the general late pagan trend towards increasing size, this type apparently persisted to form an attestedly later Anglo-Saxon type.

C_3 The largest of Anglo-Saxon leaf-shaped blades, most commonly measuring between 30 and 50 cms, present lengthier more slender profiles with the sockets taking up only something like a quarter or fifth of the length. This type has no identifiable pre-migration antecedent and seems to have developed only with the sixth century. Characteristically found with low-cone and sugar-loaf shield-bosses and objects decorated in Style II, the majority will probably have belonged to the seventh century. And this type also survives to form a familiar late Saxon type.

C_4 A small number of slender, needle-like blades might be regarded as a sub-variant of the previous type, having much the same size and proportions, but singularly attenuated, with a smooth curve running from tip to socket and no clearly identifiable junction. Associations suggest that this was a characteristically seventh-century development. But unlike the previous group, this form does not seem to have outlasted the pagan period. C_5 In Kent the type C4 is replaced by a characteristically shorter version, measuring only about 16 to 26 cms, and with a distinctive style of socketing, narrowly slit rather than decisively cleft.

D1 Throughout midland and northern England in general and in Kent - but not in Sussex or Wessex south of the Thames - small, simple leaf-shaped blades similar to those of group C1 are found on rather longer sockets, measuring in all something between 16 and 28 cms. In these the sockets are never merely burred over. Although this type has no clear pre-migration antecedent, some, like the occasional example with a welded socket, are certainly early. And unlike the short-socketed group C1, there is good evidence for its survival into the seventh century.

D2 Another type might be considered an extension of the previous form, having the blade separated from the socket by a short length of solid shank. The narrow ovoid blade deceptively appears to take up less than the two-fifths of the length it normally does. Spearheads of this type vary considerably in length between 25 and 45 cms for the most part; but some are very much longer indeed, often requiring the support of a binding-ring at the mouth of the socket. With no pre-migration antecedent and not found in any early cemeteries, this type seems only to have developed with the sixth century, and flourished especially in the later part of the sixth century and in the seventh century. But in common with other long-shanked types, probably this form did not long outlast the seventh century. Commonly found in association with Frankish-style pottery and other objects, the question of Frankish influence on this type cannot be dismissed, although the regularly cleft sockets betray insular workmanship. Its geographical distribution is distinct from that of groups D1 and 3, concentrated in Kent and along the line of the Thames - and among the Meon- and Wihtware whom we know to have had close cultural links with Kent at this time.

D3 A few spearheads present the characteristic features of the previous group in an extreme form but in rather smaller sizes, varying for the most part between 18 and 30 cms long. Smaller and proportionately broader blades are found on relatively lengthy, slender

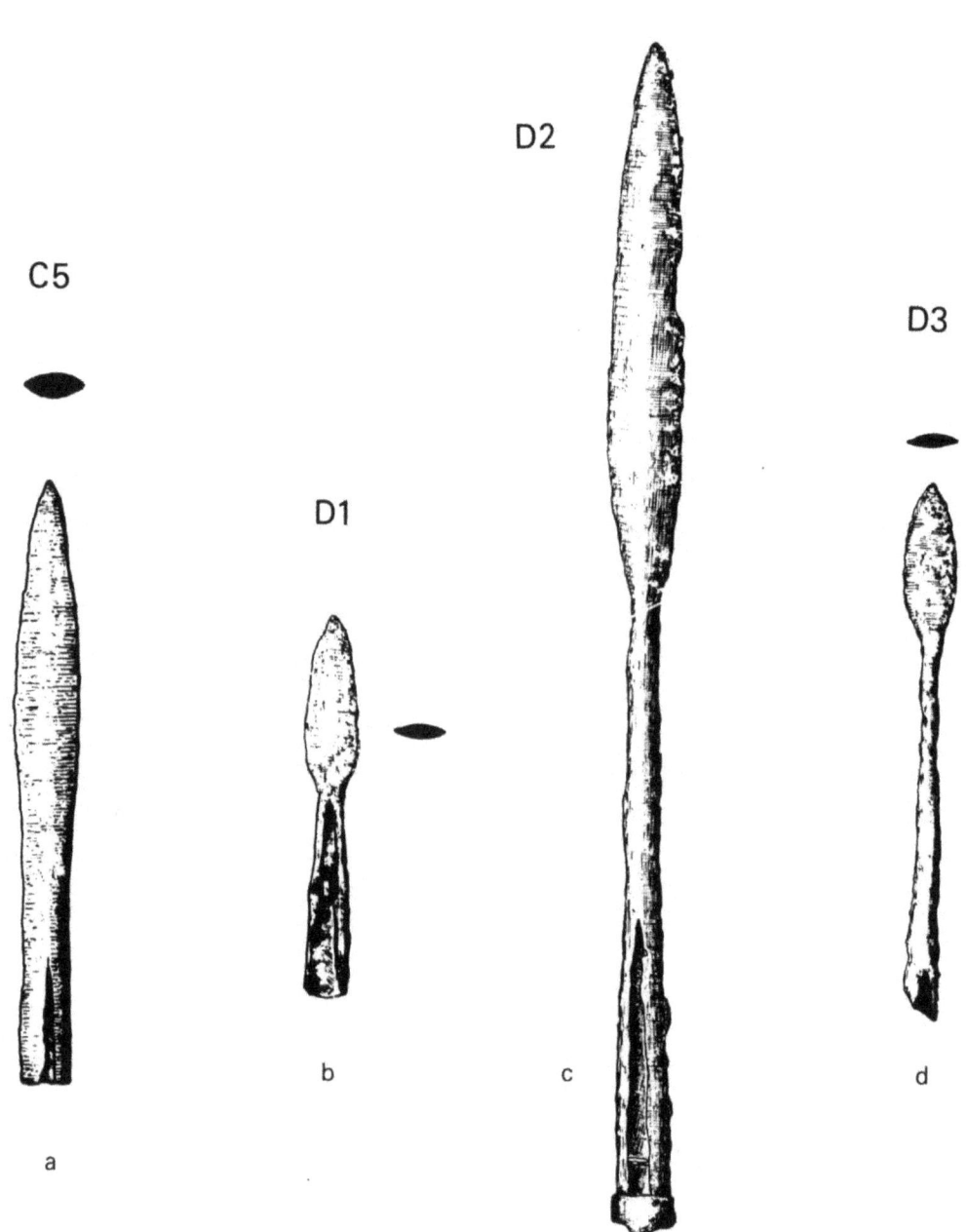

Fig. 3. a Polhill, Kent grave 84; b Linton Heath, Cambs., grave 89; c Prittlewell, Essex, grave 2; d Little Wilbraham, Cambs., Cambridge University Museum 48 1639. Scale ⅓

shanks with short cleft sockets, the distinctive profile determined largely by the flared neck. Probably all this small group belong to the sixth century. It seems not to have been related to the previous type, sharing instead a geographical distribution in common with that of group D1.

ANGULAR BLADES

Leaf-shaped blades from Anglo-Saxon graves are outnumbered many times by angular forms; although unlike the clear history that lies behind traditional Germanic leaf shapes, the exact origin of this dominant Anglo-Saxon mode is obscure, and few strictly comparable continental types were to emerge.

Series E is the angular equivalent of the leaf-shaped series C: straight-sided blades varying in size and proportion but in which the blade always represents a large part of the whole. In common with all angular profiles, these blades are invariably lozengiform in section, and regularly have their angle in the lowest part of the blade near the socket-junction.

E1 The simplest and smallest of all the angular forms, measuring from about 13 to 19 cms in length, the blade taking up half or rather more than half the whole, are found heavily distributed throughout midland England from Cambridgeshire to the Warwickshire Avon and south into the upper Thames and beyond. One or two have welded sockets and, although like the smallest leaf-shaped blades spearheads of this type tend only to come from poorly-furnished graves, such datable examples as exist indicate a relatively early phase of the settlements. There is no good evidence to suggest that many examples belonged even to the sixth century.

E2 Rather larger, if more slender blades, varying between some 20 and 35 cms in length, with the blade taking up a distinctly larger part of the whole and separated from the socket by a short solid neck, are found over very much the same area as the previous group. Like its leaf-shaped equivalent type C2, this seems to have been a long-lasting variety. Some with welded sockets come from early contexts while others have good seventh-century associations. And as with type

C2, there is good reason to believe that this type persisted into the later Anglo-Saxon period.

E3 The largest of straight-sided angular spearheads have long, tapering blades taking between two-thirds and three-quarters of the whole length, their angles close to the socket-junction. The sockets are invariably cleft up to a short solid neck. Most range from between 35 and 45 cms long, although some - especially in iron-rich areas like Kent - are very much longer. Well-dated examples are relatively rare, but as with its equivalent leaf-shaped form, the pattern seems to have been one of rapid development during the sixth century and established favour during the seventh; many are found with low-cone and sugar-loaf shield-bosses. The commonest of late pagan types, it seems strongly to have survived the abandonment of pagan funeral customs to become a characteristic late Saxon type. Scattered widely throughout the entire area of settlement, no type exhibits a broader geographical distribution - save that relatively few are found in the upper Thames.

E4 A small number of spearheads might be considered simply a particularly narrow variant of the last form: slender and delicately-made blades tapering slowly to a point, with a short cleft socket taking between a quarter and a fifth of the whole. Lengths vary between an original 30 and 50 cms. They have much the same geographical distribution as the previous type. With no pre-migration antecedent and without close continental parallel, this type seems to represent an insular development some time during the sixth century. Like its leaf-shaped counterpart type C4, there is no later Saxon form with which this might be identified.

Series F comprise small, straight-sided angular blades found on increasingly lengthy shanks. These stand in the same formal relationship *vis à vis* the lengthy angular blades of the previous series, as the long-shanked leaf-shaped series D did to the lengthy blades of series C.

F1 Small angular blades similar to those of type E1, save that now the blade-angle is often higher and more obtuse, are found on rather longer socket- and junction-pieces, the additional length bringing the

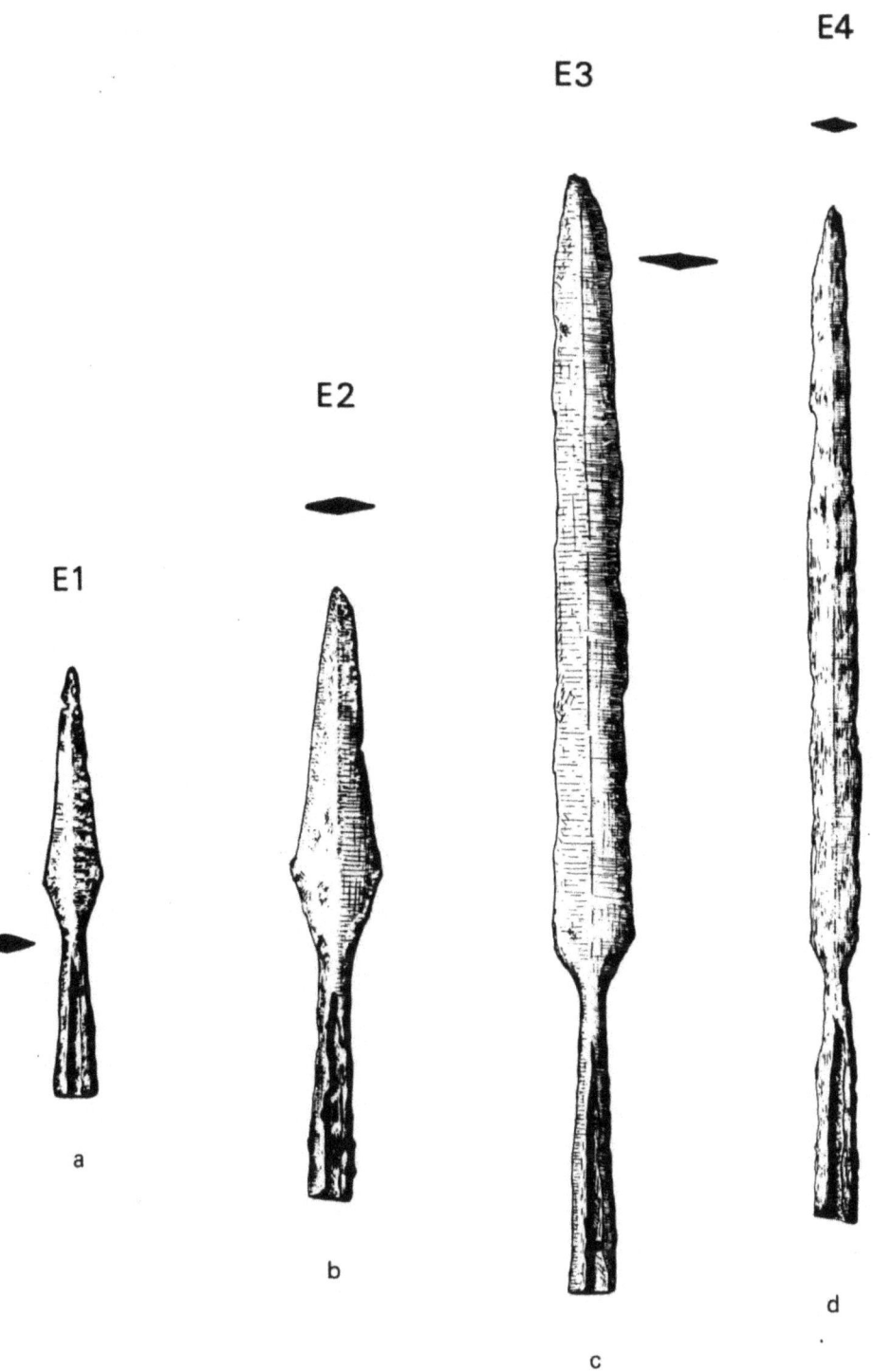

Fig. 4. a Droxford, Hants., British Museum 1902 7–22 109 ; b Woodbridge, Wilts.; c Barham, Kent, Liverpool Museum 6298; d Wrotham II, Kent. Scale ⅓

whole to between some 18 and 25 cms. Like type E1, these tend to come from only poorly-furnished graves. But similarly, there is no evidence to suggest that many lasted beyond the middle of the sixth century. As with its leaf-shaped equivalent type D1, the long socket seems to be a characteristically midland feature; spearheads of this type are found scattered generally from the Humber southwards to the Thames valley.

F2 Corresponding with leaf-shaped group D2, a small number of relatively stoutly-made spearheads seem to represent a formal extension of the previous profile, having the blade separated from the cleft socket by a length of solid shank. The majority vary between 30 and 40 cms in length. No antecedent Germanic form is known and no insular example can be given an obviously early date. As on the continent, this type seems to emerge some time during the sixth century, to find greatest favour during the seventh. They are found commonly with low-cone shield-bosses. Some examples at least, are found in association with Frankish-style objects and, as with its leaf-shaped counterpart, continental affinities for this type must certainly be recognised. But its geographical distribution is very much more widespread than that of type D2, found virtually everywhere south of the Witham. Clearly flourishing in the seventh century, there is reason to believe that this type may have survived into the eighth or ninth centuries.

F3 A small number of spearheads present the characteristic features of the previous group in an extreme form: small angular blades placed on slender solid shanks, the whole measuring about 33 or 35 cms in length. Delicately made for the most part, the characteristically slender profile is usually emphasised by the flaring neck rising to a particularly low blade-angle. Chronological evidence is slight, but as with its leaf-shaped counterpart type D3, such evidence as there is suggests that this type occurs over a distinctly earlier chronological range than that of group F2. Probably it represents a sixth-century insular development, with only the occasional survival into the seventh century. The geographical distribution of this type also seems to correspond with that of type D3.

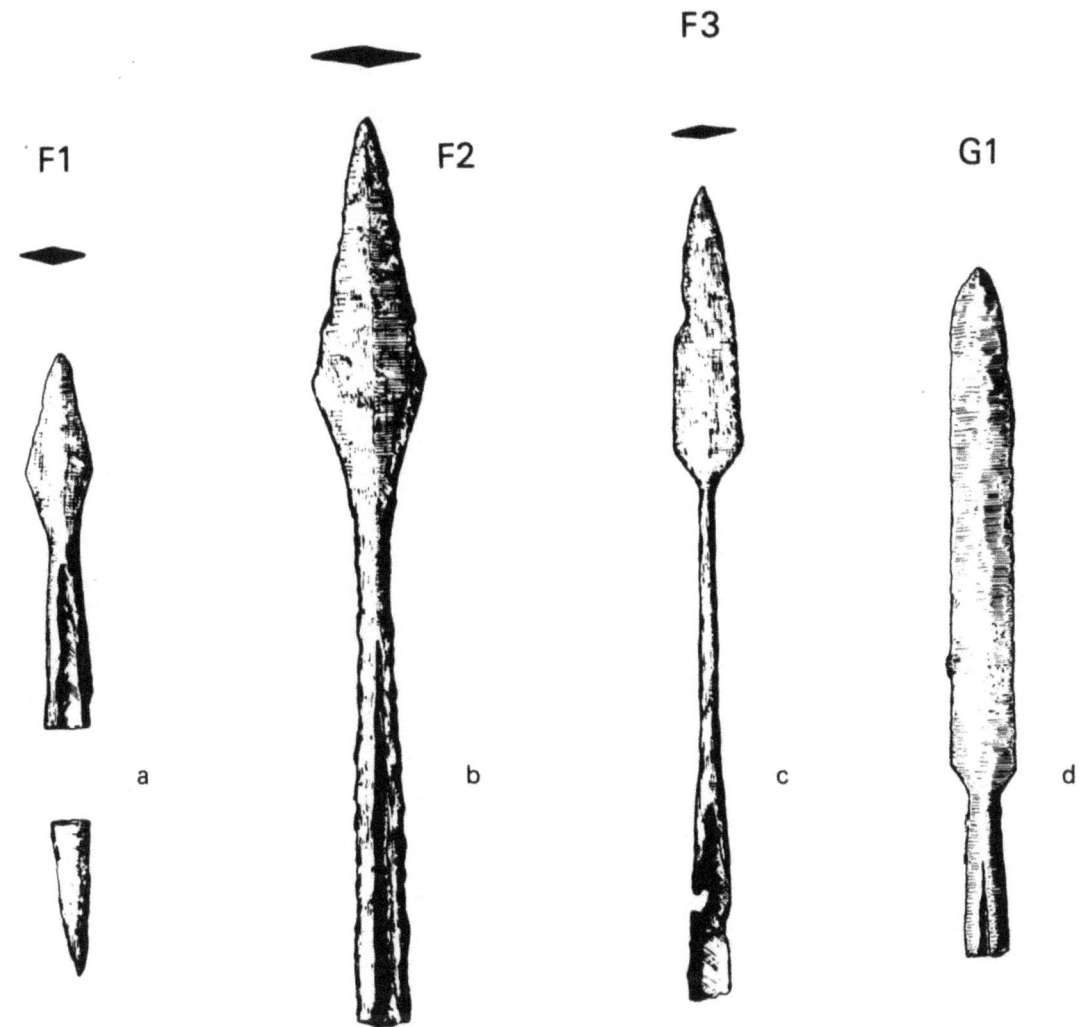

Fig. 5. a Stratford, War. grave 17; b Sibertswold, Kent, grave 23; c Brentford, Middlesex, London Museum 0.2085; d Gilton, Kent, grave A (after Douglas). Scale ⅓

Series G consists of basically sword-shaped blades, their sides noticeably parallel before pointing at the tip - a characteristic for which no clear continental parallel exists. The blade-angle is situated low down close to the socket, which normally represents about one quarter of the entire length. **G1** The smaller of the series vary in length between about 22 and 30 cms. Most have sockets cleft for their entire length; and some, from the distributional periphery, are simply burred over at the upper end. None occur in contexts that are clearly either early or late in the pagan period, and perhaps all this small group should be assigned simply some date in the sixth century. They are found thinly scattered throughout the greater part of the settlements, save that none occurs in the upper Thames, nor among the Cilternsætan or South Saxons. **G2** The larger of the series present profiles very similar to those of the smaller. Most vary between about 35 and 50 cms in length, but some are very much larger, frequently requiring the addition of a binding-ring at the mouth of the socket to support their unwieldy length. While hardly more numerous than the previous group, a relatively large number are usefully datable by association, indicating a chronological range very much that of larger blades as a whole, coming into favour only with the late sixth and seventh centuries. But unlike the large, tapering angular blades of group E3, there is no indication that this type survived the end of the seventh century. It exhibits very much the same geographical distribution as its smaller equivalent.

Series H consists of those angular blades which are distinguished by a strickening or concave curve above the angle. This feature had a long history in the Germanic north and became the 'classic' profile of the Heroic Age, commonly depicted in warrior-iconography. These are the most characteristic of all pagan Anglo-Saxon spear-types and perhaps the most popular ever, found in large numbers in all parts of the settlements. In all respects they form a singularly homogeneous group. It is convenient for the purpose of comparison with other types to divide the series into three groups by size. But alone of all types, these neither markedly increase in blade-length with overall size, (the proportions of the largest often resembling those of the smallest of the series), nor increase in size with advancing date. There are, of course, some minor differences. **H1** In the smallest blades, between some 16 and 22 cms long - far smaller than any found in Scandinavia or on the continent at this time - the characteristic concavity is often very emphatic, resulting in an almost 'winged' effect. **H2** Middle-sized examples, between about 22 and 35 cms long, are usually much more slender, sometimes with the concavity only tenuously present. **H3** Some others are very large indeed, some measuring almost 60 cms, and are

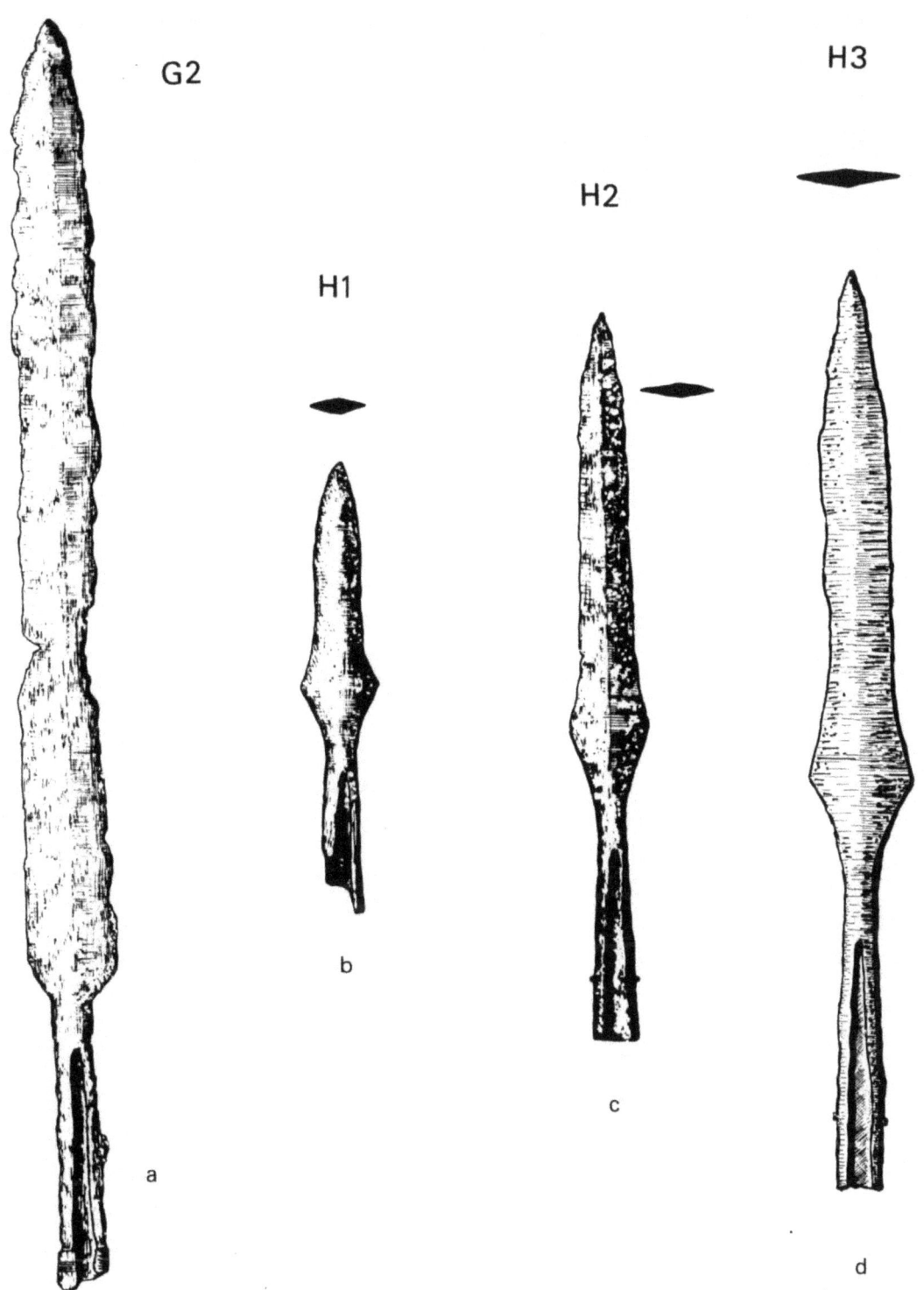

Fig. 6. a Folkestone III, Kent, grave 5; b Burford, Oxon.;
c Salisbury, Wilts.; d Sarre, Kent, grave 39. Scale ⅓

simply the most impressive blades of their time. It is no accident that spearheads of this kind characteristically accompany the richer and more remarkable sixth-century burials, and that this type commonly, almost exclusively, attracts ornament - usually taking the form of decorative wire inlays on the socket and lower blade.

The associations of this type seem uniformly early and, like its Scandinavian equivalent, blades of this kind were probably confined to the fifth and sixth centuries. None was provided with a welded socket. They are typically found with objects decorated in Jutish Style A and well-understood Style I and with moulded scabbard-mounts of the Samson-Eprave type. They are never found with shield-bosses of low-cone type, but exclusively and overwhelmingly with those of waisted and straight-carinated varieties. Probably the entire series was superseded some time during the second half of the sixth century.

CORRUGATED BLADES

Small numbers of early spearheads are found which, while presenting profiles similar to some of those described above, differ significantly in having a corrugated cross-section - either fullered or stepped. This represents a simple method of increasing longitudinal strength while economising on material and labour. It is significant that such techniques occur only in profiles where in pre-migration times mid-ribbing would have served the same purpose. Forming a distinct shadow down the centre of the blade, this insular innovation presents a strong visual, as well as convenient economic, substitute for an expensive and difficult technique which had been all but abandoned by Anglo-Saxon smiths at the time of the settlement. Characteristically associated with early glass and objects decorated in Jutish Style A and in well-understood Style I, these spearheads are probably datable as a whole to the latest fifth or earlier sixth centuries. Their development seems to have taken place during the phase of British recovery and West Saxon retrenchment which followed Mons Badonicus, *c.* 497. Localised within a limited region of Wessex south of the Thames, it seems likely that this technique was borrowed from native weapon-smiths, originating with the well-known Celtic Dark Age type illustrated by that from the Thames at Battersea (Fig. 7a).

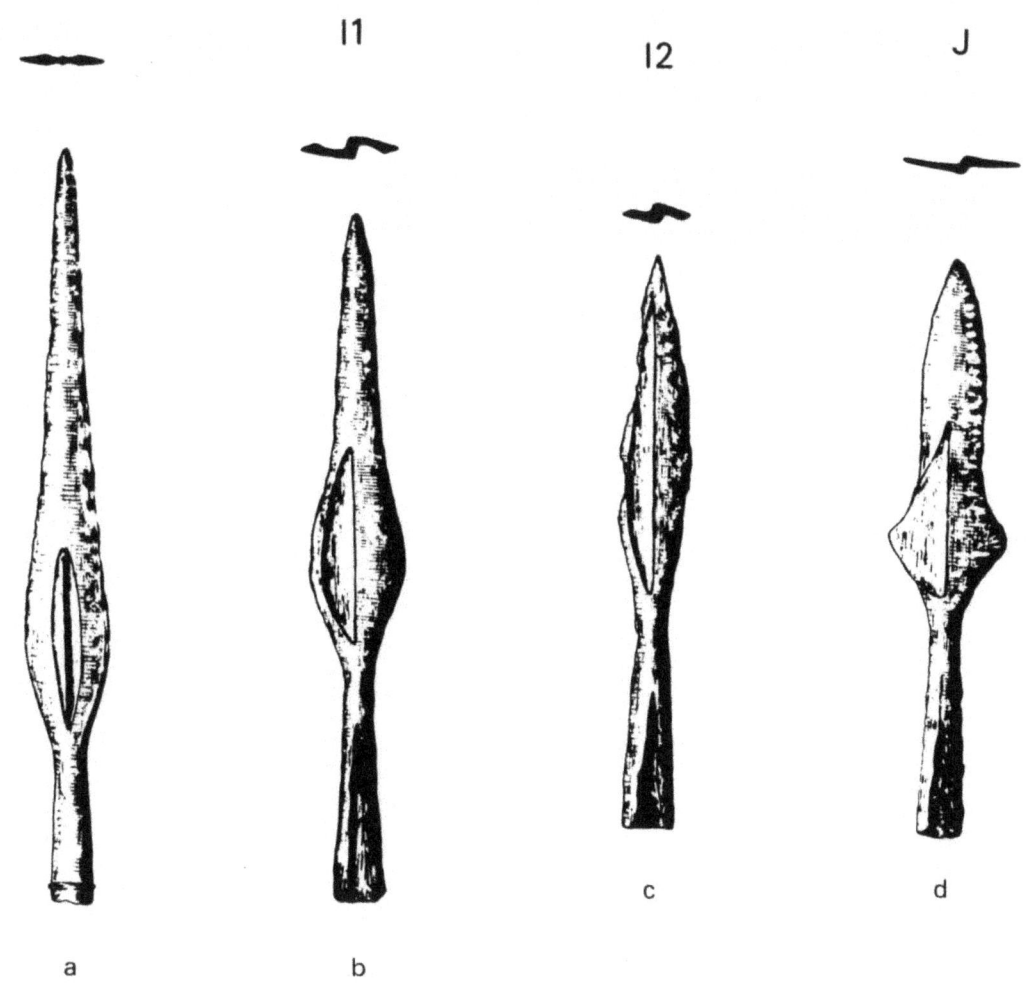

Fig. 7. a Battersea, London Museum A7347; b Droxford, Hants., British Museum 1902 7-22 90; c Brentford, Middlesex, London Museum o.2062; d Harnham Hill, Wilts., grave 14. Scale ⅓

I1 A small group of fullered blades are found with the classic La Tène profile of type B2: broad, leaf-shaped blades strickened above with a slight concavity towards the tip. The fullering, more or less broadly lunate, is contained in the left-hand lower expanded part of the blade. Their sockets are occasionally welded. Most vary between about 25 and 35 cms in length, and some narrower examples compare very closely in profile with their postulated Celtic antecedent. This type is highly localised, confined to the chalk downlands of Hampshire and limited to the north by the line of the Thames. **I2** North of the Thames, on the other hand, fullering was introduced into the other sub-variant of type B2: slender, more regularly curved leaf-shapes, a proportionately narrower fuller extending throughout the left-hand half of the blade. Sizes compare closely with those of group I1, their sockets, again occasionally welded, taking up rather less than half the whole length.

Series J Fullering of the kind found in the broad leaf-shapes of type I1 occurs also in a number of blades that might be regarded as their angular equivalent, corresponding with the concave-angular profiles of series H - the one other form to which, in Scandinavia at least, midribbing was traditional. In most examples the fullering is short and confined to the wing of the blade. Welded sockets are never found. Varying in length between some 15 and 40 cms, fullered forms cover the entire range of series H profiles except for the very largest. This type is found scattered generally through midland and southern England, also in conformity with series H, save that none have been found among the South Saxons.

K1 Another smallish group of blades present broad leaf-shaped profiles and proportions very similar to those of type I1. But in these the fullering has been beaten out so that the blade forms two plane surfaces, the left-hand half depressed, the section either severely stepped or more subtly helicoidal. The typological relationship between spearheads of this kind and those of the fullered type I1 is clear from examples in which the fullering has not been entirely beaten out at the tip of the blade. Unlike the fullered group, however, all of these spearheads have their sockets cleft in the normal Anglo-Saxon manner. The geographical distribution of this type is much that of its fullered equivalent, clearly centred on the chalk downlands south of the Thames, but rather more widely spread, with larger numbers from the upper Thames basin.

K2 North of the Thames, although still contained within a relatively limited area, with none extending into East Anglia or north of the Witham, a small number of narrower, more regularly leaf-shaped blades represent a parallel development out of fullered group I2. They cover

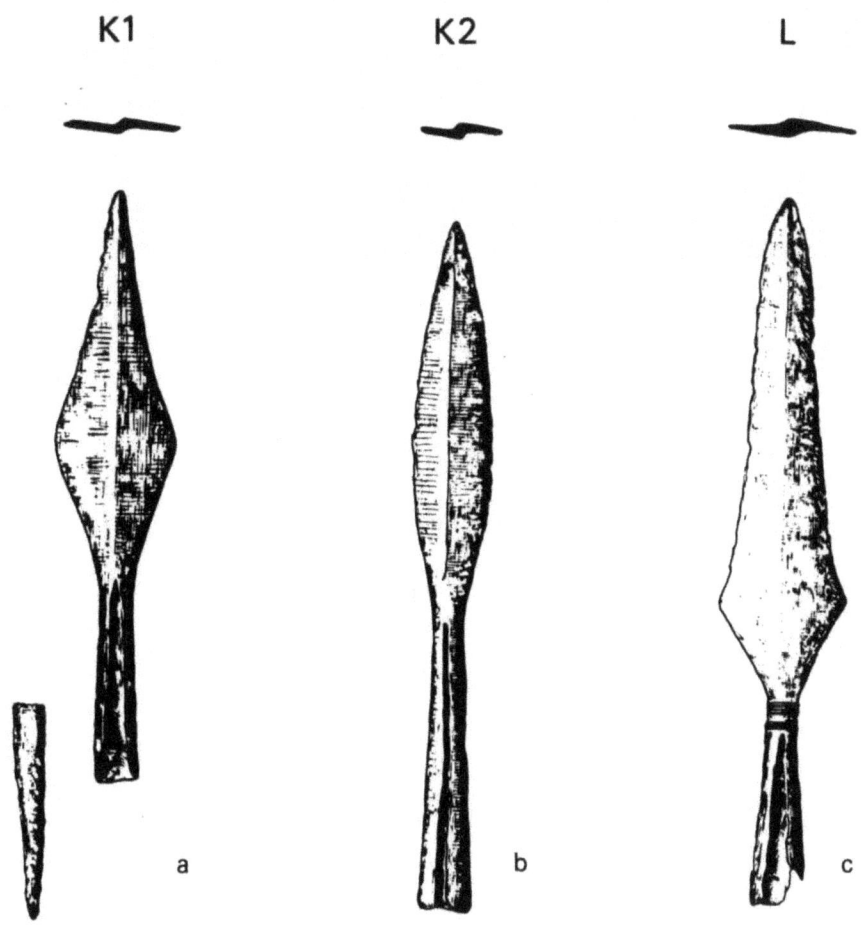

Fig. 8. a Fairford, Glos., grave 28; b Barnes, Surrey, Gunnersbury Museum o.2061; c Merrow, Surrey. Scale ⅓

a slightly smaller range of sizes than those of group I2, varying between about 16 and 30 cms in length. As with group K1, welded sockets have been entirely replaced by cleft forms; and one or two experimentally tanged examples are known. A small number of spearheads of this type found in early sixth-century contexts in nearby parts of the continent possibly represent one reflection of the set-back to West Saxon expansion that followed Mons Badonicus.

Series L Parallel with the development of the stepped section in leaf-shaped blades comes an angular equivalent in which this section was adopted into concave-angular profiles corresponding with those of the series H/J. Like series J, these cover the entire range of the original series H profiles; but, varying in length between some 20 and 35 cms, they conform for the most part with only the middle sizes of the H series. Spearheads of this kind quite commonly exhibit various types of socket-modification, such as the addition of languets, binding-rings or ornamental junction-balustering (cf. Fig. 8c). And as with the related series H, decorative inlays of different kinds are sometimes found. Like series J, the geographical distribution of this group corresponds with that of the original series H, widely scattered throughout the settlements south of the Witham.

II THE CORPUS

Site-names used conform with those listed in Audrey Meaney's *Gazetteer of Early Anglo-Saxon Burial Sites*, London, 1964. Where given lengths are preceded or followed by the letter f the spearhead concerned is incomplete at the tip or socket end respectively; where a bracket is supplied the missing portion is unlikely drastically to have affected the proportions of the object as a whole.

LIST OF ABBREVIATIONS

The majority of the abbreviated forms employed in the last column are self-explanatory; the remainder are as follows:

Abingdon	E.T. Leeds and D.B. Harden, *The Anglo-Saxon cemetery at Abingdon, Berkshire*, Oxford, 1936.
Antiquities Derbyshire	T. Bateman, *Vestiges of the Antiquities of Derbyshire*, London, 1848.
Antiquities Worcester	J. Allies, *On the Ancient British, Roman and Saxon Antiquities of Worcestershire*, 2nd ed., London, 1852.
Archaeological Index	J.Y. Akerman, *An Archaeological Index to Remains of Antiquity of the Celtic, Romano-British and Anglo-Saxon periods*, London, 1847.
Arts in Early England	G.B. Brown, *The Arts in Early England*, 2nd ed., London, 1926.
Atkinson	D. Atkinson, *The Romano-British Site on Lowbury Hill in Berkshire*, Reading, 1916.
Caistor-by-Norwich	J.N.L. Myres and B. Green, *The Anglo-Saxon Cemeteries of Caistor-by-Norwich and Markshall, Norfolk*, London, 1973.

Cambridge Region	C.F. Fox, *The Archaeology of the Cambridge Region*, Cambridge, 1923.
Collectanea Antiqua	C.R. Smith, *Collectanea Antiqua*, London, 1848-80.
Defence Sites	W.F. Grimes et al., *Excavations on Defence Sites, 1939-45*, vol. I, London, 1960.
Discoveries at Broadstairs	H. Hurd, *Some Notes on recent archaeological discoveries at Broadstairs*, Broadstairs, 1913.
Earthworks of the New Forest	H. Sumner, *The Ancient Earthworks of the New Forest*, London, 1917.
Fairford Graves	W.M. Wylie, *Fairford Graves. A record of researches in an Anglo-Saxon burial place*, Oxford, 1852.
Faussett Papers	Unpublished Faussett MSS in Liverpool Public Museum and the collection of The Society of Antiquaries of London.
Forty Years' Researches	J.R. Mortimer, *Forty Years' Researches in British and Saxon Burial Mounds of East Yorkshire*, London, 1905.
Inventorium Sepulchrale	B. Faussett, *Inventorium Sepulchrale*, ed. C.R. Smith, London, 1856.
JBAA.	*Journal of the British Archaeological Association.*
London & the Saxons	R.E.M. Wheeler, *London and the Saxons*, London, 1935.
Nenia Britannica	J. Douglas, *Nenia Britannica*, London, 1793.
Petersfinger	E.T. Leeds and H. de S. Shortt, *An Anglo-Saxon Cemetery at Petersfinger, near Salisbury, Wilts.*, Salisbury, 1953.
PPSEA.	*Proceedings of the Prehistoric Society of East Anglia.*
PSA.	*Proceedings of The Society of Antiquaries of London.*
PSA. Newc.	*Proceedings of the Society of Antiquaries of Newcastle upon Tyne.*
PSAS.	*Proceedings of the Society of Antiquaries of Scotland.*

Richborough IV	J.P. Bushe-Fox, *Fourth Report on the Excavations of the Roman Fort at Richborough, Kent*, London, 1949.
Richborough V	B.W. Cunliffe, ed., *Fifth Report on the Excavations of the Roman Fort at Richborough, Kent*, London, 1968.
Saxon Obsequies	R.C. Neville, *Saxon Obsequies*, London, 1852.
Spearheads	M.J. Swanton, *The Spearheads of the Anglo-Saxon Settlements*, London, 1973.
Ten Years' Diggings	T. Bateman, *Ten Years' Diggings in Celtic and Saxon Grave Hills in the counties of Derby, Stafford and York from 1848-1858*, London, 1861.
West Kent	B. Philp, *Excavations in West Kent 1960-1970*, Dover, 1973.
Williams-Freeman	J.P. Williams-Freeman, *An Introduction to Field Archaeology as illustrated by Hampshire*, London, 1915.

Provenance	Nature of find.	Type Length	Butt-ferrule	Associated weapons.	Museum Accession no.	Publication
Abingdon I Berks.	grave 4	H1 f18.8	-	shield	Ashmolean Museum	*Abingdon*, 32, pl.xviii.
Abingdon I Berks.	grave 10	H2 21.8	-	knife	Ashmolean Museum	*Abingdon*, 33, pl.xviii.
Abingdon I Berks.	grave 11	H2 f20.2	-	shield	Ashmolean Museum	*Abingdon*, 33, pl.xviii.
Abingdon I Berks.	grave 21	F1 f14.7	-	-	Ashmolean Museum	*Abingdon*, 35, pl.xviii.
Abingdon I Berks.	grave 22	H2 23.5	conical 9.6	knife	Ashmolean Museum	*Abingdon*, 35, pl.xviii.
Abingdon I Berks.	grave 25	H2 23.2	-	knife, shield	Ashmolean Museum	*Abingdon*, 35, pl.xviii.
Abingdon I Berks.	grave 33	H3 37.3	-	knife, shield	Abingdon Museum	*Abingdon*, 37, pl.xviii.
Abingdon I Berks.	grave 35a	E1 14.0	-	-	Ashmolean Museum	*Abingdon*, 37.
Abingdon I Berks.	grave 39	F1 17.3	-	knife, shield	Ashmolean Museum	*Abingdon*, 38, pl.xviii.
Abingdon I Berks.	grave 39	E1 15.5	-	knife, shield	Ashmolean Museum	*Abingdon*, 38, pl.xviii.
Abingdon I Berks.	grave 48	K1 33.3	-	knife, shield	Ashmolean Museum	*Abingdon*, 40, pl.xviii.
Abingdon I Berks.	grave 49	K1 f25.5	conical 8.9	knife, sword	Ashmolean Museum	*Abingdon*, 40, pl.xviii.
Abingdon I Berks.	grave 52	H2 f19.6	-	knife	Ashmolean Museum	*Abingdon*, 41.
Abingdon I Berks.	grave 55	K1 f26.7	conical 8.2	knife, shield	Ashmolean Museum	*Abingdon*, 41, pl.xviii.
Abingdon I Berks.	cremation burial 67	-	conical 6.8	-	Ashmolean Museum	*Abingdon*, 21, pl.iii.
Abingdon I Berks.I	grave 69	A1 35.5	*	knife, shield	Abingdon Museum	*Abingdon*, 44, pl.xviii.
Abingdon I Berks.I	grave 69	A2 52.7	*	knife, shield	Abingdon Museum	*Abingdon*, 44, pl.xviii.
Abingdon I Berks.	grave 73	H2 25.4	-	-	Ashmolean Museum	*Abingdon*, 45, pl.xviii.
Abingdon I Berks.	grave 77	E1 14.3	-	knife	Ashmolean Museum 1934 234.2	*Abingdon*, 46.
Abingdon I Berks.	grave 83	E1 15.5	-	knife	Ashmolean Museum	*Abingdon*, 47.
Abingdon I Berks.	grave 111	I2 26.9	-	knife	Ashmolean Museum	*Abingdon*, 52.
Abingdon I Berks.	grave	E3 33.8f	-	2 knives	Ashmolean Museum 1935 738	-
Abingdon I Berks.	-	E3 f27.3	-	-	Ashmolean Museum	-
Abingdon I Berks.	-	H2 f26.1	-	-	Ashmolean Museum	-
Abington Pigotts, Cambs-	?grave	E3 f31.6f	-	knife	Cambridge University 51 317b	-
Acklam Wold Yorks.	grave	-	tubular 1.8	knife, sword	-	*Forty Years' Researches*, 94, fig. 226.
Alcester Warwicks.	-	C2 33.5	-	-	Birmingham Museum	-
Alfriston Susses	grave 36a	L f21.0	-	-	-	*Sussex Arch.Collections*, LVI, 1914, 37, pl.20.8.
Alfriston Sussex	grave 54	F2 f24.6f	-	shield	Lewes Museum	*Sussex Arch.Collections*, LVI, 1914, 43, pl.20,10.
Alfriston Sussex	grave 63	C1 11.1f	-	-	-	*Sussex Arch.Collections*, LVI, 1914, 45, pl.20,6.
Alfriston Sussex	grave E	H2 f19.8f	-	3 knives	Lewes Museum	*Sussex Arch.Collections*, LVI, 1914, 49, pl.20,2.
Alfriston Sussex	grave H	H3 f35.5	-	larger and smaller knives	Lewes Museum	*Sussex Arch.Collections*, LVI, 1914, 50, pl.20,7.
Alfriston Sussex	grave U1	C4 f39.0	-	-	Lewes Museum	*Spearheads*, fig. 15a.

Provenance	Nature of find.	Type Length	Butt-ferrule	Associated weapons.	Museum Accession no.	Publication
Alfriston Sussex	grave U2	F2 f30.1	-	-	Lewes Museum	-
Alfriston Sussex	grave	E3 33.1f	-	-	Lewes Museum	-
Alfriston Sussex	grave	H2 19.4(f	-	-	Toronto Museum 924.60	-
Alfriston Sussex	grave	E2 f22.3	-	-	Toronto Museum 924.60	-
Alresford Hants.	Roman Villa	D1 f17.4f	-	-	Colchester Museum 1.85	-
Alton Hants.	grave 16	E2 26.4	-	knife, shield, sword	Alton Museum	Antiqu.Journal, XLIII, 1963, 43, fig. 19c.
Alton Hants.	grave 16	F1 f)20.4	-	knife, shield, sword	Alton Museum	Antiqu.Journal, XLIII, 1963, 43, fig. 20a.
Alton Hants.	grave	G1 22.0	-	-	Alton Museum 1959.62	-
Alton Hants.	grave	E4 37.7f	-	-	Alton Museum 1959.63	-
Alton Hants.	grave	H2 24.0	-	-	Alton Museum 1959.103	-
Alton Hants.	grave	K1 f)39.5	conical 9.2	-	Alton Museum 1959.104-5	-
Alton Hants.	grave	L f)32,5	-	-	Alton Museum OC.952	-
Alton Hants.	grave	F2 f)32.0	-	-	Alton Museum	-
Alvediston Wilts.	grave	E3 f28.5	* 7.5	shield	Devizes Museum 103	Wilts.Arch.Magazine, XXXVII, 1912, 435.
Appleby Lincs.	-	H2 27.6	-	-	Scunthorpe Museum	-
Ashdown Berks.	-	E1 14.4	-	-	British Museum 55 10-18 3	-
Aston Berks.	grave	L 21.6f	-	"other weapons"	British Museum 82 2-20 2	Spearheads, 213.
Aston Berks.	grave	H3 f27.5f	-	-	British Museum 87 11-12 4	-
Aston Berks.	grave	K2 24.8	-	-	British Museum 87 11-12 5	-
Aston Berks.	grave	E1 f13.7f	-	-	British Museum 87 11-12 6	-
Aston Berks.	grave	L f28.1	-	-	British Museum 87 11-12 7	-
Aston Berks.	grave	F2 f29.3	-	-	British Museum 87 11-12 8	-
Aston Berks.	grave	L f23.3f	-	-	British Museum	-
Aston Berks.	grave	H3 f24.0(f	-	-	British Museum	-
Aston Tirrold Berks.	grave	E1 22.5	-	-	Ashmolean Museum 1887 2552	-
Astwick Beds.	grave	E4 42.3	-	-	British Museum 1915 12-8 350	Trans.Herts.Field Club, IV, 1886, 40, pl. 2.
Astwick Beds.	grave	C2 f25.5f	-	-	British Museum 1915 12-8 351	-
Astwick Beds.	grave	E1 17.8(f	-	-	British Museum 1915 12-8 352	-
Astwick Beds.	grave	C2 24.4(f	-	-	British Museum 1915 12-8 355	-
Astwick Beds.	grave	C3 33.7f	-	-	British Museum 1915 12-8 356	-
Astwick Beds.	grave	C2 28.7(f	-	-	British Museum 1915 12-8 357	-
Astwick Beds.	grave	F3 f28.6f	-	-	British Museum 1915 12-8 359	Spearheads, fig. 34b.

Provenance	Nature of find.	Type Length	Butt-ferrule	Associated weapons.	Museum Accession no.	Publication
Aylesford Kent	grave	F2 f16.8f	-	-	Maidstone Museum	*Spearheads*, 185.
Aylesford Kent	grave	G2 f17.2f	-	-	Maidstone Museum	*Spearheads*, 185, 189.
Aylesford Kent	grave	E3 32.7f	-	-	Maidstone Museum	-
Aylesford Kent	grave	D2 f16.3f	-	-	Maidstone Museum	-
Aylesford Kent	grave	D2 f31.0	-	-	Maidstone Museum	-
Aylesford Kent	grave	E3 37.5f	-	-	Maidstone Museum	-
Aynho Oxon.	-	C3 f41.1f	-	-	Northampton Museum D221 1955-6	-
Badbury Rings Dorset	surface	E1 19.4f	-	-	British Museum 92 9-1 1564	-
Badwell Ash Suffolk	grave	L f22.2f	-	-	Ipswich Museum 1935 100	-
Badwell Ash Suffolk	grave	F2 f27.6	-	-	Ipswich Museum 1935 100	-
Badwell Ash Suffolk	grave	E4 31.4	-	-	Ipswich Museum 1935 100	-
Badwell Ash Suffolk	grave	H3 f)37.2(f	-	-	Ipswich Museum 1935 100	-
Badwell Ash Suffolk	grave	H3 f)40.3	-	-	Ipswich Museum 1935 100	-
Badwell Ash Suffolk	grave	E3 f34.4	-	-	Ipswich Museum 1935 100	-
Baggrave Leics.	grave	H2 30.0	-	shield	-	*Nenia Britannica*, 27, pl. vii,2,
Baginton Warwicks.	grave	E4 f31.0f	-	-	Coventry Museum	-
Baginton Warwicks.	grave	E3 f24.0f	-	-	Coventry Museum	-
Baginton Warwicks	grave	H2 f23.9f	-	-	Coventry Museum	-
Baginton Warwicks.	grave	H1 22.1f	-	-	Coventry Museum	-
Baginton Warwicks.	grave	E4 f36.1f	-	-	Coventry Museum	-
Baginton Warwicks.	grave	H3 f30.4f	-	-	Coventry Museum	*Antiqu.Journal*, XXXVIII, 1958, 240, pl, 27b.
Baginton Warwicks.	grave	E4 f34.2f	-	-	Coventry Museum	-
Baginton Warwicks.	grave	E3 40.6f	-	-	Coventry Museum	-
Baginton Warwicks.	grave	H1 15.7f	-	-	Coventry Museum	-
Baginton Warwicks.	grave	E1 10.3(f	-	-	Coventry Museum	-
Baginton Warwicks	grave	L 24.1	-	-	Coventry Museum	-
Baginton Warwicks.	grave	H3 f34.4	-	-	Coventry Museum	*Antiqu.Journal*, XXXVIII, 1958, 240, pl. 27b.
Baginton Warwicks.	grave	H1 20.8	-	-	Coventry Museum	-
Baginton Warwicks.	grave	E1 f15.3	-	-	Coventry Museum	-
Baginton Warwicks.	grave	F1 f14.2	-	-	Coventry Museum	-
Baginton Warwicks.	grave	E3 f27.6(f	-	-	Coventry Museum	-
Baginton Warwicks.	grave	E4 f19.2(f	-	-	Coventry Museum	-
Baginton Warwicks.	grave	H2 27.8	-	-	Coventry Museum	-

Provenance	Nature of find.	Type Length	Butt-ferrule	Associated weapons.	Museum Accession no.	Publication
Baginton Warwicks.	grave	C2 f)24.5	-	-	Coventry Museum	-
Baginton Warwicks.	grave	F1 12.0	-	-	Coventry Museum	-
Baginton Warwicks.	grave	C1 20.0	-	-	Coventry Museum	-
Baginton Warwicks.	grave	E2 f20.1	-	-	Coventry Museum	-
Baginton Warwicks.	grave	H3 f29.7	-	-	Coventry Museum	-
Baginton Warwicks.	grave	F1 15.3	-	-	Coventry Museum	-
Baginton Warwicks	grave	L f)23.7	-	-	Coventry Museum	-
Baginton Warwicks	grave	H1 f)19.3	-	-	Coventry Museum	-
Baginton Warwicks.	grave	H2 20.7	-	-	Coventry Museum	-
Bantham Devon	settlement site	F1 f10.9	-	-	Torquay Museum	Antiqu.Journal, XXXV, 1955, 61, fig.4.
Bantham Devon	settlement site	F1 10.7	-	-	Torquay Museum	Antiqu.Journal, XXXV, 1955, 61, fig.4.
Barbury Castle Wilts.	-	E2 f18.2f	-	-	Ashmolean Museum 1955 364	-
Barbury Castle Wilts.	-	E2 f17.7f	-	-	Ashmolean Museum 1955 364	-
Barham Kent	grave	E3 f43.1	-	-	Liverpool Museum 6296	Spearheads, fig. 27a.
Barham Kent	grave	E4 f)50.4(f	-	-	Liverpool Museum 6297	-
Barham Kent	grave	E3 f46.6	-	-	Liverpool Museum 6298	Spearheads, fig. 27b,
Barham Kent	grave	E3 46.5	-	-	Liverpool Museum 6315	-
Barham Kent	grave	F2 30.9	-	-	Liverpool Museum 6316	-
Barham Kent	grave	C2 f24.0	-	-	Liverpool Museum 6319	-
Barham Kent	grave	C1 14.0f	-	-	Liverpool Museum 6320	-
Barham Kent	grave	F3 f25.0f	-	-	Liverpool Museum 6321	-
Barnes Surrey	River Thames	K2 29.9	-	-	Gunnersbury Park Museum, 0,2061	Spearheads, fig. 52b.
Barnes Surrey	River Thames	C5 f)18.2f	-	-	London Museum A17175	-
Barrington A Cambs.	grave 3	H2 26.5	-	-	-	Collectanea Antiqua, VI, 157, pl. 29,5.
Barrington A Cambs.	grave 7	H3 29.0	-	-	-	Collectanea Antiqua, VI, 158.
Barrington A Cambs.	grave 12	C3 35.5	-	-	-	Collectanea Antiqua, VI, 159, pl. 29,8.
Barrington A Cambs.	grave 14	G2 40.5	-	knife	-	Collectanea Antiqua, VI, 159, pl. 29,9.
Barrington A Cambs.	grave 16	H3 33.0	-	shield	-	Collectanea Antiqua, VI, 160, pl. 29,7.
Barrington A Cambs.	grave 18	H3	-	knife	-	Collectanea Antiqua, VI, 160, pl. 29,1.
Barrington A Cambs.	grave 22a	H3	-	knife	-	Collectanea Antiqua, VI, 160, pl. 29,2.
Barrington A Cambs.	grave 22b	D1	-	knife	-	Collectanea Antiqua, VI, 160, pl. 29,3.
Barrington A Cambs.	grave 26	D1	-	knife	-	Collectanea Antiqua, VI, 161, pl. 29,4.
Barrington A Cambs.	grave	H3 34.7	-	-	British Museum 76 2-12 49	Spearheads, fig. 41b.

Provenance	Nature of find.	Type Length	Butt-ferrule	Associated weapons.	Museum Accession no.	Publication
Barrington A Cambs.	grave	H2 27.6	-	-	British Museum 76 2-12 50	-
Barrington A Cambs.	grave	H2 22.7	-	-	British Museum 76 2-12 51	-
Barrington A Cambs.	grave	H1 17.9	-	-	British Museum 76 2-12 52	-
Barrington B Cambs.	grave	H2 22.4	-	-	Exeter University History Department	-
Barrow Hill Wilts.	grave	F2 f)30.0	-	shield	Devizes Museum 14	Wilts.Arch.Magazine, XLIII, 1925, 101, fig.3.
Barrow on Soar Leics.	-	D1 f14.6f	-	-	Leicester Museum 5.1903	-
Barrow on Soar Leics.	-	H3 31.3	-	-	Leicester Museum 5.1903	-
Basingstoke Hants.	grave	B2 f)26.2(f	-	-	Basingstoke Museum OC.861	Spearheads, 41, fig, 7d.
Bassett Down Wilts.	grave	C1 14.4	-	knife, shield	Devizes Museum 16	Wilts.Arch.Magazine, XXVIII, 1896, 104, fig.
Bassett Down Wilts.	grave	I1 27.3	-	knife, shield	Devizes Museum 21	Wilts.Arch.Magazine, XXVIII, 1896, 105, fig.
Battersea London	River Thames	B2 53.2	-	-	British Museum 52 5-4 1	-
Battersea London	River Thames	I2 f8.2f	-	-	British Museum 58 5-14 1	-
Battersea London	River Thames	F2 25.6(f	-	-	British Museum 61 6-20 6	-
Battersea London	River Thames	I2 22.2f	-	-	London Museum A8840	London & the Saxons, 168, pl.x,4.
Battersea London	River Thames	F2 26.4	-	-	London Museum A15462	London & the Saxons, 163, pl.ix,7.
Beakesbourne I Kent	grave 28	F2 c38.0	-	knife	-	Faussett Papers.
Beakesbourne II Kent	grave 1	D1 f)13.8(f	-	-	Canterbury Museum RM.7585	-
Beakesbourne II Kent	grave 2	E3 f)32.0	conical 8.9	-	Canterbury Museum RM.7593-4	-
Beakesbourne II Kent	grave 3	H3 51.9	-	-	Canterbury Museum RM.7597	Spearheads, 203, fig. 80a.
Beakesbourne II Kent	grave 4	E2 27.4	-	-	Canterbury Museum RM.7601	-
Beakesbourne II Kent	grave 5	J 29.9	-	-	Canterbury Museum RM.7603	-
Bedale Yorks.	?grave	B1	-	-	-	JBAA., V, 1849, 220.
Beddington Surrey	grave	C2 21.4	-	-	Guildford Museum S.8977	-
Beddington Surrey	grave	L f)27.0f	-	-	Guildford Museum S.8979	-
Beddington Surrey	grave	E4 43.2	-	-	Guildford Museum S.8980	-
Beddington Surrey	grave	C3 29.4	-	-	Guildford Museum S.8981	Spearheads, fig, 11b.
Beddington Surrey	-	C1 f13.4	-	-	Guildford Museum RB.1012	-
Beddington Surrey	-	H1 17.3	-	-	Guildford Museum RB.1012	Spearheads, fig, 37a.
Beddington Surrey	-	C3 24.2f	-	-	Guildford Museum RB.1012	-
Beddington Surrey	-	A2 f15.0f	-	-	Guildford Museum RB.1012	-
Beddington Surrey	-	F3 f)35.1(f	-	-	Guildford Museum RB.1012	-
Beddington Surrey	-	E4 26.8f	-	-	Guildford Museum RB.1012	-
Bedford Beds.	-	H2 24.2	-	-	Bedford Museum 3810	-

Provenance	Nature of find.	Type Length	Butt-ferrule	Associated weapons.	Museum Accession no.	Publication
Bedford Beds.	-	J 22.6	-	-	Bedford Museum 3811	-
Benson Oxon.	River Thames	F2 f)17.2	-	-	Ashmolean Museum 1942 244	-
Benson Oxon.	River Thames	I2 36.0	-	-	Reading Museum 228.62	-
Bidford Warwicks.	grave 163	C1 15.7	-	knife	Stratford Museum	Archaeologia, LXXIV, 1923-4, 285.
Bidford Warwicks.	grave 183	H1 f)14.9	-	knife, another spear	Stratford Museum	Archaeologia, LXXIV, 1923-4, 287.
Bidford Warwicks.	grave	C3 32.8f	-	-	-	Archaeologia, LXXIII, 1922-3, pl.x.
Bidford Warwicks.	grave	C2 f)29.6	-	-	-	Archaeologia, LXXIII, 1922-3, pl.x.
Bidford Warwicks.	grave	H2 28.2	-	-	-	Archaeologia, LXXIII, 1922-3, pl.x.
Bidford Warwicks.	grave	H2 23.2f	-	-	-	Archaeologia, LXXIII, 1922-3, pl.x.
Bidford Warwicks.	grave	E2 24.5	-	-	-	Archaeologia, LXXIII, 1922-3, pl.x.
Bidford Warwicks.	grave	E2 24.0	-	-	-	Archaeologia, LXXIII, 1922-3, pl.x.
Bidford Warwicks.	grave	H1 17.2	-	-	-	Archaeologia, LXXIII, 1922-3, pl.x.
Bidford Warwicks.	grave	D1 21.7	-	-	Stratford Museum	-
Bidford Warwicks.	grave	H2 f21.3	-	-	Stratford Museum	-
Bidford Warwicks.	grave	H2 24.2	-	-	Stratford Museum	-
Bidford Warwicks.	grave	D1 24.5	-	-	Stratford Museum	-
Bidford Warwicks.	grave	H2 27.0	-	-	Stratford Museum	-
Bidford Warwicks.	grave	E1 14.5(f	-	-	Stratford Museum	-
Bidford Warwicks	grave	E1 f)18.6(f	-	-	Stratford Museum	-
Bidford Warwicks.	grave	E1 15.2(f	-	-	Stratford Museum	-
Bidford Warwicks.	grave	H1 f)15.8	-	-	Stratford Museum	-
Bidford Warwicks.	grave	H1 14.2(f	-	-	Stratford Museum	-
Bidford Warwicks.	grave	E1 12.4(f	-	-	Stratford Museum	-
Bidford Warwicks.	grave	E1 f)18.6(f	-	-	Stratford Museum	-
Bidford Warwicks.	grave	H1 f)15.8	-	-	Stratford Museum	-
Bidford Warwicks.	grave	C1 12.8(f	-	-	Stratford Museum	-
Bidford Warwicks.	grave	H1 14.3(f	-	-	Stratford Museum	-
Bidford Warwicks.	grave	E1 14.2(f	-	-	Stratford Museum	-
Bidford Warwicks.	grave	L 21.3	-	-	Stratford Museum	-
Bidford Warwicks.	grave	C3 32.8	-	-	Stratford Museum	-
Bidford Warwicks.	grave	E2 f)19.5(f	-	-	Stratford Museum	-
Bidford Warwicks.	grave	C4 f)26.0(f	-	-	Stratford Museum	-
Bidford Warwicks.	grave	H3 f)36.6	-	-	Stratford Museum	-

Provenance	Nature of find.	Type Length	Butt-ferrule	Associated weapons.	Museum Accession no.	Publication
Bidford Warwicks.	grave	E2 f)21.4(f	-	-	Stratford Museum	-
Bidford Warwicks.	grave	E2 18.2(f	-	-	Stratford Museum	-
Bidford Warwicks.	grave	E3 35.8(f	-	-	Stratford Museum	-
Bidford Warwicks.	grave	E2 f)25.0	-	-	Stratford Museum	-
Bifrons Kent	grave 43	H3 f)44.2f	*	knife, seax, another spear.	Maidstone Museum 875	Arch.Cantiana, X, 1876, 315.
Bifrons Kent	grave 66	C3 34.1	-	knife	Maidstone Museum 894	Arch.Cantiana, XIII, 1880, 554.
Bifrons Kent	grave	A1 f)24.3	-	-	Maidstone Museum 620	Spearheads, 31, fig. 4e.
Bifrons Kent	grave	D2 f)70.2	-	-	Maidstone Museum 620	-
Bifrons Kent	grave	G1 36.1	-	-	Maidstone Museum 620 1954 23	-
Bifrons Kent	grave	H3 51.1	-	-	Maidstone Museum 620 1954 24	-
Bifrons Kent	grave	C2 31.3	-	-	Maidstone Museum 620 1954 25	-
Bifrons Kent	grave	H3 45.1	-	-	Maidstone Museum 620 1954 26	-
Bifrons Kent	grave	H3 40.6	-	-	Maidstone Museum 620 1954 27	-
Bifrons Kent	grave	G2 f32.3f	-	-	Maidstone Museum 620 1954 28	-
Bifrons Kent	grave	E2 f.19.0f	-	-	Maidstone Museum 620 1954 29	-
Bifrons Kent	grave	D2 57.2	-	-	Maidstone Museum 811	Spearheads, fig. 20e.
Bifrons Kent	grave	E3 51.6	-	-	Maidstone Museum 872	-
Bifrons Kent	grave	H3 55.0	-	-	Maidstone Museum 873	-
Bifrons Kent	grave	E3 42.8	-	-	Maidstone Museum 877	-
Bifrons Kent	grave	H3 41.7	-	-	Maidstone Museum 882	-
Bifrons Kent	grave	H3 31.2	-	-	Maidstone Museum 890	-
Bifrons Kent	grave	E3 35.7	-	-	Maidstone Museum 891	-
Bifrons Kent	grave	H3 31.9	-	-	Maidstone Museum 892	-
Bifrons Kent	grave	C3 33.7	-	-	Maidstone Museum 902	-
Bifrons Kent	grave	L 21.1f	-	-	Maidstone Museum 907	-
Bifrons or Sarre Kent	grave	A2 f31.4	-	-	Maidstone Museum 870	-
Bifrons or Sarre Kent	grave	A2 f)30.2f	-	-	Maidstone Museum 870	-
Bifrons or Sarre Kent	grave	A2 f50.8f	-	-	Maidstone Museum 889	-
Bifrons or Sarre Kent	grave	H3 34.6	-	-	Maidstone Museum 904	-
Bifrons or Sarre Kent	grave	C2 f20.7	-	-	Maidstone Museum 905	-
Bifrons or Sarre Kent	grave	H3 f)25.9f	-	-	Maidstone Museum 913	-
Bifrons or Sarre Kent	grave	E2 22.1(f	-	-	Maidstone Museum 914	-
Bifrons or Sarre Kent	grave	E2 17.3f	-	-	Maidstone Museum 917	-

Provenance	Nature of find.	Type Length	Butt-ferrule	Associated weapons.	Museum Accession no.	Publication
Bifrons or Sarre Kent	grave	G1 27.0	-	-	Maidstone Museum 919	-
Bifrons or Sarre Kent	grave	A2 f68.3f	-	-	Maidstone Museum	-
Bifrons or Sarre Kent	grave	G2 f17.9f	-	-	Maidstone Museum	-
Bifrons or Sarre Kent	rave	G2 f9.9f	-	-	Maidstone Museum	-
Bifrons or Sarre Kent	grave	F2 f16.7f	-	-	Maidstone Museum	-
Bifrons or Sarre Kent	grave	H2 f17.2f	-	-	Maidstone Museum	-
Bifrons or Sarre Kent	grave	F2 14.2f	-	-	Maidstone Museum	-
Bifrons or Sarre Kent	grave	F2 f)17.6f	-	-	Maidstone Museum	-
Bifrons or Sarre Kent	grave	L f17.3f	-	-	Maidstone Museum	-
Bifrons or Sarre Kent	grave	G2 f23.3f	-	-	Maidstone Museum	-
Bifrons or Sarre Kent	grave	C3 f20.6f	-	-	Maidstone Museum	-
Bifrons or Sarre Kent	grave	E3 f29.9	-	-	Maidstone Museum	-
Bifrons or Sarre Kent	grave	E3 f28.2	-	-	Maidstone Museum	-
Bifrons or Sarre Kent	grave	F3 f23.6f	-	-	Maidstone Museum	-
Bifrons or Sarre Kent	grave	H3 f23.5	-	-	Maidstone Museum	-
Bifrons or Sarre Kent	grave	C2 f)28.3	-	-	Maidstone Museum	-
Bifrons or Sarre Kent	grave	D2 f)25.6	-	-	Maidstone Museum	-
Bifrons or Sarre Kent	grave	E3 f19.2	-	-	Maidstone Museum	-
Bifrons or Sarre Kent	grave	C2 30.2	-	-	Maidstone Museum	-
Bifrons or Sarre Kent	grave	E3 46.3	-	-	Maidstone Museum	-
Bigbury Kent	-	D2 f)21.5(f	-	-	Toronto Museum 927 66.20	-
Bigbury Kent	-	E3 48.8	-	-	Toronto Museum 927 66.22	-
Birstall Leics.	-	H2 f23.9f	-	-	Leicester Museum 155 1958.8	-
Bishopstone Bucks.	grave	E3 41.8	-	-	Aylesbury Museum 5.80	-
Bishopstone Bucks.	grave	H1 18.2	-	-	Aylesbury Museum 6.80	-
Bishopstone Bucks.	grave	F1 19.7	-	-	Aylesbury Museum 7.80	-
Bishopstone Bucks.	grave	L 28.8	-	-	Aylesbury Museum 8.80	-
Bishopstone Bucks.	grave	H2 18.8	-	-	Aylesbury Museum 9.80	-
Bishopstone Bucks.	grave	L 18.1f	-	-	Aylesbury Museum 13.80	-
Blakeney Glos.	-	E3 30.4f	-	-	Gloucester Museum A1109	-
Blewburton Hill Berks.	grave 7	H2 21.6	-	knife	Reading Museum	Berks.Arch.Journal, LIII, 1953, 21, fig. 20,2.
Blisworth Northants.	-	E2 25.2f	-	-	British Museum 82 6-12 152	-
Blockley Worcs.	grave 1	H1 18.5	-	knife, shield	Ashmolean Museum 1924 935	Trans.Worcs.Arch.Soc., III, 1925, 128, pl.

Provenance	Nature of find.	Type Length	Butt-ferrule	Associated weapons.	Museum Accession no.	Publication
Blockley Worcs.	grave 3	A2 f13.0f	-	-	Ashmolean Museum 1925 561	Trans.Worcs.Arch.Soc., III, 1925, 128, pl.
Blockley Worcs.	grave	H1 18.7	-	-	Ashmolean Museum 1935 258	-
Boscombe Down Wilts.	grave	E2 28.0f	-	-	Salisbury Museum	-
Bottisham Cambs.	-	C3 31.3	-	-	Cambridge Museum 42.28	-
Boughton Aluph Kent	grave	E3 43.0	-	shield	-	Nenia Britannica, 121, pl. xxv.
Boxford Berks.	-	L 11.4f	-	-	Newbury Museum	-
Boxley Kent	grave	C3 f29.0(f	-	-	Maidstone Museum 365.8	-
Boxley Kent	grave	D2 f26.7	-	-	Maidstone Museum	-
Boxley Kent	grave	E2 f20.8f	-	-	Maidstone Museum	-
Breach Down Kent	grave	C1	-	-	-	Archaeological Index, 135, pl.xv,12.
Bredon's Norton Worcs.	grave	H2 30.6	-	-	-	Antiquities Worcester, 76-8, pl.iii.
Bredon's Norton Worcs.	grave	H2 24.8	-	-	-	Antiquities Worcester, 76-8, pl.iii.
Bredon's Norton Worcs.	grave	H1 17.4	-	-	-	Antiquities Worcester, 76-8, pl.iii.
Bredon's Norton Worcs.	grave	H1 12.6	-	-	-	Antiquities Worcester, 76-8, pl.iii.
Bredon's Norton Worcs.	grave	H1 15.6	-	-	-	Antiquities Worcester, 76-8, pl.iii.
Brentford Middlesex	River Thames	C3 32.0	-	-	London Museum A9625	-
Brentford Middlesex	River Thames	L 12.5f	-	-	London Museum A13582	-
Brentford Middlesex	River Thames	C2 13.5f	-	-	London Museum A13583	-
Brentford Middlesex	River Thames	I1 30.0f	-	-	London Museum A13597	London & the Saxons, 168, pl.x,3.
Brentford Middlesex	River Thames	I2 27.8(f	-	-	London Museum A13598	London & the Saxons, 168, pl.x,2.
Brentford Middlesex	River Thames	I2 24.1	-	-	London Museum A13835	London & the Saxons, 168.
Brentford Middlesex	River Thames	B2 20.0f	-	-	London Museum O.1775	-
Brentford Middlesex	River Thames	B2 28.5	-	-	London Museum O.1783	-
Brentford Middlesex	River Thames	B2 30.3(f	-	-	London Museum O.1784	Spearheads, fig. 7a.
Brentford Middlesex	River Thames	B2 22.0	-	-	London Museum O.1786	-
Brentford Middlesex	River Thames	C1 f)17.4	-	-	London Museum O.1788	-
Brentford Middlesex	River Thames	H3 21.8f	-	-	London Museum O.1790	-
Brentford Middlesex	River Thames	I1 26.7f	-	-	London Museum O.1790	-
Brentford Middlesex	River Thames	H3 21.4f	-	-	London Museum O.1790	-
Brentford Middlesex	River Thames	E3 20.5f	-	-	London Museum O.1790	-
Brentford Middlesex	River Thames	E3 36.4	-	-	London Museum O.2030	-
Brentford Middlesex	River Thames	L 26.8	-	-	London Museum O.2031	-
Brentford Middlesex	River Thames	H2 27.6	-	-	London Museum O.2032	-

Provenance	Nature of find.	Type Length	Butt-ferrule	Associated weapons.	Museum Accession no.	Publication
Brentford Middlesex	River Thames	H2 27.6	-	-	London Museum 0.2032	-
Brentford Middlesex	River Thames	H1 18.2	-	-	London Museum 0.2033	-
Brentford Middlesex	River Thames	H3 47.3	-	-	London Museum 0.2040	-
Brentford Middlesex	River Thames	E4 55.8	-	-	London Museum 0.2047	-
Brentford Middlesex	River Thames	C2 24.4	-	-	London Museum 0.2054	-
Brentford Middlesex	River Thames	C1 22.6	-	-	London Museum 0.2055	-
Brentford Middlesex	River Thames	K2 36.7	-	-	London Museum 0.2060	*Spearheads*, fig. 52a.
Brentford Middlesex	River Thames	J f15.6f	-	-	London Museum 0.2061	-
Brentford Middlesex	River Thames	E3 40.5f	-	-	London Museum 0.2062	-
Brentford Middlesex	River Thames	I2 24.6	-	-	London Museum 0.2062	*Spearheads*, fig. 47b.
Brentford Middlesex	River Thames	I2 25.0	-	-	London Museum 0.2063	-
Brentford Middlesex	River Thames	J 39.6	-	-	London Museum 0.2065	*Spearheads*, fig. 48d.
Brentford Middlesex	River Thames	L 29.2(f	-	-	London Museum 0.2074	-
Brentford Middlesex	River Thames	L f)38.4	-	-	London Museum 0.2082	-
Brentford Middlesex	River Thames	B2 33.0	-	-	London Museum 0.2084	-
Brentford Middlesex	River Thames	B2 f)27.0	-	-	London Museum 0.2085	-
Brentford Middlesex	River Thames	F1 20.8	-	-	London Museum 0.2086	-
Brentford Middlesex	River Thames	F2 f)18.9(f	-	-	London Museum 0.2086	-
Brentford Middlesex	River Thames	F2 18.1	-	-	London Museum 0.2086	-
Brentford Middlesex	River Thames	C2 15.4	-	-	London Museum 0.2086	-
Brentford Middlesex	River Thames	D3 f)15.3(f	-	-	London Museum 0.2086	-
Brentford Middlesex	River Thames	E1 f)9.4(f	-	-	London Museum 0.2086	-
Brentford Middlesex	River Thames	F2 f18.9	-	-	London Museum 0.2086	-
Brentford Middlesex	River Thames	F1 f)10.9(f	-	-	London Museum 0.2087	-
Brentford Middlesex	River Thames	B2 f)16.5(f	-	-	London Museum 0.20133	-
Brentford Middlesex	River Thames	B2 41.6	-	-	Toronto Museum FA.23	*Eurasia Sept.Antiqua*, IX, 1934, 392, pl.vii.
Brettenham-Bridgham, Norfk.	grave	C2 40.1	-	shield	Norwich Museum 5.934	*Norfolk Archaeology*, XXVI, 1937, 128-9.
Brighthampton Oxon.	grave 2	K1 26.8	conical 11.7	knife	Ashmolean Museum 1966.6	*Archaeologia*, XXXVII, 1857, 393-4.
Brighthampton Oxon.	grave 3	E1 20.5	-	knife	Ashmolean Museum	*Archaeologia*, XXXVII, 1857, 394.
		E1 11.0	-		Ashmolean Museum	*Archaeologia*, XXXVII, 1857, 394.
Brighthampton Oxon.	grave 13	H2 24.9	-	knife, shield	Ashmolean Museum	*Archaeologia*, XXXVII, 1857, 395.
Brighthampton Oxon.	grave 31	H1 f15.4	-	knife, sword	Ashmolean Museum	*Archaeologia*, XXXVIII, 1858, 87.
Brighthampton Oxon.	grave 44	H1 f)21.2	-	knife, sword	Ashmolean Museum	*Archaeologia*, XXXVIII, 1858, 89.

Provenance	Nature of find.	Type Length	Butt-ferrule	Associated weapons.	Museum Accession no.	Publication
Brighthampton Oxon.	grave 50	H1 f)15.0	-	knife	Ashmolean Museum	*Archaeologia*, XXXVIII, 1858, 89.
Brighton Sussex	grave	E2 f)18.9(f	-	sword, shield	Alnwick Castle 281	*Sussex Arch.Collections*, II, 1849, 269.
Brighton Sussex	grave	B2 27.7	-	-	Brighton Museum	*Arts in Early England*, III, 235, pl. 32,4.
Brixworth Northants.	grave	H2 27.7	-	-	Northampton Museum D.244	-
Brixworth Northants.	grave	E1 17.7	-	-	Northampton Museum D.245	-
Brixworth Northants.	grave	C2 20.1(f	-	-	Northampton Museum D.246	-
Brixworth Northants.	grave	E1 f)20.1(f	-	-	Northampton Museum D.254	-
Brixworth Northants.	grave	E1 f)20.0	-	-	Northampton Museum D.255	-
Brixworth Northants.	grave	L 23.0	-	-	Northampton Museum D.256	-
Brixworth Northants.	grave	K2 f)23.4	-	-	Northampton Museum D.257	-
Brixworth Northants.	grave	D1 21.9(f	-	-	Northampton Museum D.258	-
Brixworth Northants.	grave	H1 f)20.1	-	-	Northampton Museum D.259	-
Brixworth Northants.	grave	E1 17.3	-	-	Northampton Museum D.260	-
Brixworth Northants.	grave	H2 f)22.9	-	-	Northampton Museum D.261	-
Brixworth Northants.	grave	F2 16.6(f	-	-	Northampton Museum D.262	-
Brixworth Northants.	grave	E1 13.0	-	-	Northampton Museum D.263	-
Brixworth Northants.	grave	H1 18.5	-	-	Northampton Museum D.264	-
Brixworth Northants.	grave	J f)15.3(f	-	-	Northampton Museum D.265	-
Brixworth Northants.	grave	D3 24.0	-	-	Northampton Museum D.266	-
Brixworth Northants.	grave	H3 32.5	-	-	Northampton Museum D.267	-
Brixworth Northants.	grave	C2 29.9	-	-	Northampton Museum D.268	-
Brixworth Northants.	grave	H3 f)25.1(f	-	-	Northampton Museum D.269	-
Brixworth Northants.	grave	J 23.6	-	-	Northampton Museum D.275	-
Brixworth Northants.	grave	E2 24.7	-	-	Northampton Museum D.276	-
Brixworth Northants.	grave	E3 f)33.8(f	-	-	Northampton Museum D.277	-
Brixworth Northants.	grave	C4 f44.8f	-	-	Northampton Museum D.278	-
Brixworth Northants.	grave	E4 f46.3(f	-	-	Northampton Museum D.279	-
Brixworth Northants.	grave	C4 f)41.7(f	-	-	Northampton Museum D.280	-
Brixworth Northants.	grave	H3 37.8	-	-	Northampton Museum D.281	-
Broad Chalke Wilts.	grave 1	H3 f)39.6	-	-	Devizes Museum 122	*Wilts.Arch.Magazine*, XLIII, 1927, 94, fig.4,
Broad Chalke Wilts.	grave 3	G1 f18.2f	-	-	Devizes Museum 124	*Wilts.Arch.Magazine*, XLIII, 1927, 94,
Broad Chalke Wilts.	grave 5	H2 f)28.8	-	shield	Devizes Museum 126	*Wilts.Arch.Magazine*, XLIII, 1927, 94.
Broadstairs Kent	grave	D1 f21.4f	-	seax, shield	Broadstairs Museum	*Discoveries at Broadstairs*, 23.

Provenance	Nature of find.	Type Length	Butt-ferrule	Associated weapons.	Museum Accession no.	Publication
Broadstairs Kent	grave 1	E2 33.7	-	knife	British Museum	-
Broadstairs Kent	grave 2	E3 43.0	-	knife	British Museum	*Spearheads*, 179.
Broadway Worcs.	grave	H2 22.7	-	?shield	-	*Antiqu.Journal*, XXXVIII, 1958, 58, fig. 9.
Broadwell Glos.	grave	C3 44.8	-	-	Bristol Museum	*Trans.Bristol & Glos.A.S.*, LXXXIII, 1964, 13, fig.1s.
Brooke Norfolk	grave	E2 f21.6f	-	-	British Museum 70 11-5 25	-
Brooke Norfolk	grave	H2 f)22.8f	-	-	British Museum 70 11-5 26	-
Brooke Norfolk	grave	G1 f16.6f	-	-	British Museum 70 11-5 27	-
Brooke Norfolk	grave	E3 f26.1	-	-	British Museum 70 11-5 28	-
Brooke Norfolk	grave	H2 27.0	-	-	British Museum 70 11-5 29	-
Brooke Norfolk	grave	F1 23.3	-	-	British Museum 70 11-5 30	*Spearheads*, fig. 31b.
Brooke Norfolk	grave	E2 f)24.9	-	-	British Museum 70 11-5 31	-
Brooke Norfolk	grave	E1 15.3	-	-	British Museum 70 11-5 32	-
Brooke Norfolk	grave	F2 f)22.9	-	-	British Museum 70 11-5 33	-
Brooke Norfolk	grave	E1 f19.0(f	-	-	British Museum 70 11-5 34	-
Broomfield Essex	grave	E4 f14.3f	-	knife, sword, shield	British Museum 95 12-16 7	*Trans.Essex Arch.Soc.*, NS.V, 1895, 250.
Bulford Wilts.	?grave	C1 f)13.7	-	-	Salisbury Museum 79.38	*Wilts.Arch.Magazine*, XLVIII, 1939, 352.
Bungay Suffolk	grave 1	E2 f27.0	-	-	-	*Proc.Suffolk Arch.Inst.*, XXV, 1951, 304, fig.17a.
Burford Oxon.	grave	H1 21.1	-	sword, shield	British Museum 48 7-27 3	*Oxoniensia*, XXXIV, 1969, 113-4, fig. 21e.
		H2 f26.2	-		British Museum 48 7-27 4	*Oxoniensia*, XXXIV, 1969, 113-4.
Burn Ground Glos.	grave 6	L 33.9	-	knife	Gloucester Museum A.2587	*Defence Sites I*, 120-21, fig. 50.
Burn Ground Glos.	grave 9	C1 f14.2	-	-	Gloucester Museum A.2593	*Defence Sites I*, 124, fig. 50.
Burn Ground Glos.	grave 10	L f18.5	-	knife	Gloucester Museum A.2595	*Defence Sites I*, 124, fig. 50.
Burrough Hill Leics.	-	E3 26.8f	-	-	Leicester Museum 24.1892	-
Burrough Hill Leics.	-	E3 f)40.4(f	-	-	Leicester Museum 32.1862	-
Bury St Edmunds I Suffolk	grave	E3 f25.0f	-	shield	Bury St Edmunds K.43	*Antiqu.Journal*, XLIII, 1963, 43, fig. 18e.
Bury St Edmunds II Suffolk	grave	H2 f25.4	-	shield	Bury St Edmunds K.62	-
Buttsole Kent	?grave	E3 36.5f	-	-	Huddersfield Museum	-
Buttsole Kent	grave	E2 17.2f	-	-	Maidstone Museum	-
Buttsole Kent	grave	C1 f)10.0f	-	-	Maidstone Museum	-
Buttsole Kent	grave	E2 f12.3f	-	-	Maidstone Museum	-
Buttsole Kent	grave	G1 f)24.1	-	-	Maidstone Museum	-
Caistor-by-Norwich, Norfk	grave 3	E3 f40.1	-	knife	Norwich Museum 77.939	*Caistor-by-Norwich*, 215, 219, fig. 60.
Caistor-by-Norwich, Norfk	grave 10	H3 36.1	conical 9.1	knife, shield	Norwich Museum 77.939	*Caistor-by-Norwich*, 215, 222, fig. 61.

Provenance	Nature of find.	Type Length	Butt-ferrule	Associated weapons.	Museum Accession no.	Publication
Cambridge I Cambs.	grave 1	C2 16.5	-	-	-	Proc.Cambridge Ant.Soc., XVI, 1912, 122, pl.xii.
Cambridge I Cambs.	grave	H3 44.0	-	-	Cambridge Museum	-
Cambridge II Cambs.	grave	H2 f)28.0	cylindrical 2.0	-	Ashmolean Museum 1886 1384	-
Cambridge II Cambs.	grave	C1 f)14.3	-	-	Ashmolean Museum 1886 1386	-
Cambridge II Cambs.	grave	H1 f18.7f	-	-	Cambridge Museum 1901 189a	-
Cambridge II Cambs.	grave	H3 36.5	-	-	Ashmolean Museum 1928 485	-
Cambridge II Cambs.	grave	L f)25.2	-	-	Ashmolean Museum 1928 486	-
Cambridge Cambs.	River Cam	E2 f)20.6f	-	-	Cambridge Museum	-
Carvoran Northumberland	Roman Fort	A1 55.0	-	-	Newcastle Museum 1956 265a	PSA.Newc., 4thS, IX, 1939-41, 136-8, pl.v.
Cassington I Oxon.	grave 1	C2 21.5	conical 5.5	knife, shield, another spear.	Ashmolean Museum 1942 161	Oxoniensia, VII, 1942, 61.
Cassington I Oxon.	grave 6	H1 f)18.4	-	knife	Ashmolean Museum	Oxoniensia, VII, 1942, 61.
Cassington II Oxon.	?grave	J 24.1	-	-	Ashmolean Museum 1945 122	-
Cassington II Oxon.	?grave	H2 23.4	-	-	Ashmolean Museum 1951 126	Oxoniensia, XVI, 1951, 79.
Castle Hill Edinburgh	-	F1 f)18.0(f	-	axe	Edinburgh Museum HH.340	PSAS., LIII, 1918-9, 129.
Catterick Yorks.	grave	H2 f)23.8(f	-	-	York Museum 1961 7	-
Caythorpe Lincs.	-	H3 f33.2f	-	-	Grantham Museum AS.40	-
Caythorpe Lincs.	-	E3 f)31.8(f	-	-	Grantham Museum AS.41	-
Caythorpe Lincs.	-	J f)20.4f	-	-	Grantham Museum AS.42	-
Caythorpe Lincs.	-	C2 f11.4(f	-	-	Grantham Museum AS.60	-
Caythorpe Lincs.	-	H2 15.4f	-	-	Grantham Museum AS.62	-
Charnage Mere Wilts.	surface find	E2 f14.4f	-	-	Salisbury Museum	Wilts.Arch.Magazine, XLVI, 1934, 173.
Chartham Down Kent	grave 39	F1 13.2	-	-	-	Inventorium Sepulchrale, 173, fig.
Chatham Lines Kent	grave 3	F2 37.0	-	knife, shield	-	Nenia Britannica, 11, fig. 1.
Chatham Lines Kent	grave 16	C2 22.0	-	knife	-	Nenia Britannica, 56, pl. xiii,5.
Chatteris Cambs.	grave	C2 c26.0	-	sword, shield	-	Gentleman's Magazine, XXXVI, 1766, 119, fig.
Cheam Surrey	surface find	E2 30.3	-	-	-	Surrey Arch.Collections, LI, 1949, 151-2, fig.
Cherbury Camp Berks.	surface find	E1 f)17.7f	-	-	Ashmolean Museum 1955 364d	-
Cherry Hinton Cambs.	grave 1	C2 20.8	-	knife	Cambridge Museum 53.117	-
Chessell Down IOW.	grave	J 45.8	-	-	British Museum 69 10-11 19	-
Chessell Down IOW.	grave	H3 42.7	-	-	British Museum 69 10-11 20	-
Chessell Down IOW.	grave	H3 f40.1	-	-	British Museum 69 10-11 21	-
Chessell Down IOW.	grave	C3 f)39.3	-	-	British Museum 69 10-11 22	-
Chessell Down IOW.	grave	E3 f32.4(f	-	-	British Museum 69 10-11 23	-

Provenance	Nature of find.	Type Length	Butt-ferrule	Associated weapons.	Museum Accession no.	Publication
Chessell Down IOW.	grave	H3 28.6	-	-	British Museum 69 10-11 24	-
Chessell Down IOW.	grave	E3 f31.1	-	-	British Museum 69 10-11 25	-
Chessell Down IOW.	grave	L f29.2(f	-	-	British Museum 69 10-11 26	-
Chessell Down IOW.	grave	H2 f24.2	-	-	British Museum 69 10-11 27	-
Chessell Down IOW.	grave	H2 f)25.4	-	-	British Museum 69 10-11 28	-
Chessell Down IOW.	grave	H2 f19.9f	-	-	British Museum 69 10-11 29	-
Chessell Down IOW.	grave	L f)22.2	-	-	British Museum 69 10-11 30	-
Chessell Down IOW.	grave	H1 f19.5	-	-	British Museum 69 10-11 31	-
Chessell Down IOW.	grave	F1 21.6	-	-	British Museum 69 10-11 32	-
Chessell Down IOW.	grave	H1 19.7	-	-	British Museum 69 10-11 33	-
Chessell Down IOW.	grave	H2 f20.9(f	-	-	British Museum 69 10-11 34	-
Chessell Down IOW.	grave	H1 f19.7(f	-	-	British Museum 69 10-11 35	-
Chessell Down IOW.	grave	L f)23.9	-	-	British Museum 69 10-11 36	-
Chessell Down IOW.	grave	C2 f22.3	-	-	British Museum 69 10-11 37	-
Chessell Down IOW.	grave	C1 18.8	-	-	British Museum 69 10-11 38	*Spearheads*, fig. 9e.
Chessell Down IOW.	grave	D2 f)24.7(f	-	-	British Museum 69 10-11 39	*Spearheads*, fig. 20a.
Chessell Down IOW.	grave	E4 42.6(f	-	-	Newport Museum	-
Chessell Down IOW.	grave	C3 f)21.0(f	-	-	Newport Museum	-
Chilbolton Wilts. Hants	?grave	L f22.5	-	shield	Salisbury Museum	Williams-Freeman, 423.
Chiswick Middlesex	River Thames	H3 27.7	-	-	London Museum 0.2052	-
Chiswick Eyot Middlesex	River Thames	H1 17.1	-	-	London Museum A23335	*London & the Saxons*, 163, pl. ix,5.
Churchover Warwicks.	grave	C1 16.6	-	-	Leicester Museum 2 1946	-
Churchover Warwicks.	grave	H1 f13.9	-	-	Leicester Museum 2 1946	-
Churchover Warwicks.	grave	H2 21.5	-	-	Leicester Museum 2 1946	-
Churchover Warwicks.	grave	H1 17.8	-	-	Warwick Museum A.11	-
Churchover Warwicks.	grave	H2 21.9f	-	-	Warwick Museum A.11	-
Churchover Warwicks.	grave	H2 21.0f	-	-	Warwick Museum A.11	-
Churchover Warwicks.	grave	H2 24.9	-	-	Warwick Museum A.11	-
Churchover Warwicks.	grave	H2 25.8	-	-	Warwick Museum A.11	-
Churchover Warwicks.	grave	H3 f)31.8	-	-	Warwick Museum A.11	-
Churchover Warwicks.	grave	H3 f)37.7	-	-	Warwick Museum A.11	-
Churchover Warwicks.	grave	L 21.0	-	-	Warwick Museum A.11	-
Churchover Warwicks.	grave	G2 37.9f	-	-	Warwick Museum A.11	-

Provenance	Nature of find.	Type Length	Butt-ferrule	Associated weapons.	Museum Accession no.	Publication
Churchover Warwicks.	grave	C2 20.6f	-	-	Warwick Museum A.11	-
Cleat Hill Beds.	?grave	K2 26.0	-	-	Bedford Museum 3886	-
Clipston Northants.	grave	C2 f20.1	-	knife, seax	Northampton Museum D.216	*Spearheads*, 157.
Cliveden Bucks.	River Thames	C1 18.5	-	-	Reading Museum 280.47	-
Colchester Essex	-	E2 25.2	-	-	Colchester Museum	-
Colchester Essex	-	C3 f27.0f	-	-	Colchester Museum	-
Colchester Essex	-	H1 19.5	-	-	Colchester Museum	-
Colchester Essex	-	E4 f34.8f	-	-	Colchester Museum	-
Colchester Essex	-	B2 10.2	-	-	Colchester Museum	-
Colchester Essex	-	C2 f12.3f	-	-	Colchester Museum	-
Colchester Essex	-	F1 f14.0	-	-	Colchester Museum	-
Colchester Essex	-	H3 32.2f	-	-	Colchester Museum	-
Colchester Essex	-	B1 16.1	-	-	Colchester Museum	-
Colchester Essex	-	C1 f)13.9(f	-	-	Colchester Museum	-
Colchester Essex	grave	C1 17.7(f	-	-	Colchester Museum PC mdx-xiii	*Spearheads*, fig. 9f.
Colchester Essex	grave	H2 23.1	-	shield	Colchester Museum PC mdx-xiii	-
Colchester Essex	grave	D1 f)25.3	-	-	Colchester Museum PC mdx-xiii	-
Colchester Essex	grave	E3 38.1(f	-	shield	Colchester Museum PC.1508	-
		G2 28.3(f	-		Colchester Museum PC.1509	-
Colchester Essex	surface find	C1 f10.9	-	-	Colchester Museum 640.36	-
Colchester Essex	-	C1 f)13.4f	-	-	Colchester Museum 3609.17	-
Colchester Essex	-	C2 f)15.9	-	-	Colchester Museum	-
Compton Pauncefoot, Somerset	grave	C4 f37.8f	-	shield	Taunton Museum 66.A.67	*Proc.Somerset Arch.Soc.*, CXI, 1967, 68-9,
Cookham Berks.	River Thames	D1 f)36.0(f	-	-	Hull Museum	-
Cookham Berks.	River Thames	I2 f23.8	-	-	Reading Museum 28.31	-
Cop Round Barrow Bucks.	grave 2	C1 14.0	-	knife	-	*Records of Bucks.*, XIII, 1938, 336, fig.
Cotgrave Notts.	grave	C2 f)20.4	-	-	Sheffield Museum J93.1132	*JBAA.*, VIII, 1853, 190.
		H3 f)35.8(f	-	-	Sheffield Museum J93.1134	*JBAA.*, VIII, 1853, 190.
Cotgrave Notts.	grave	H3 f17.6f	-	another spear	Sheffield Museum J93.1137	*JBAA.*, VIII, 1853, 190.
Cross Barrow Berks.	grave 3	C2	-	shield, another spear	-	*PSA.*, 2ndS. XV, 1895, 328.
Croydon Surrey	grave	A2 96.0(f	-	-	-	-
Croydon Surrey	grave	B2 41.6	-	-	British Museum 95 3-13 17	-
Croydon Surrey	grave	H3 36.7(f	-	-	British Museum 95 3-13 18	-

Provenance	Nature of find.	Type Length	Butt-ferrule	Associated weapons.	Museum Accession no.	Publication
Croydon Surrey	grave	E3 f)38.6	-	-	British Museum 95 3-13 19	-
Croydon Surrey	grave	E2 f)25.4(f	-	-	British Museum 95 3-13 20	-
Croydon Surrey	grave	C3 f)38.9	-	-	British Museum 95 3-13 21	-
Croydon Surrey	grave	E4 f)30.7f	-	-	British Museum 95 3-13 22	-
Croydon Surrey	grave	C2 22.8	-	-	British Museum 95 3-13 23	-
Croydon Surrey	grave	H2 19.1f	-	-	British Museum 95 3-13 24	-
Croydon Surrey	grave	H1 18.2	-	-	British Museum 95 3-13 25	-
Croydon Surrey	grave	F1 f18.0	-	-	British Museum 95 3-13 26	-
Croydon Surrey	grave	F1 f)23.5	-	-	British Museum 95 3-13 27	-
Croydon Surrey	grave	E1 15.7	-	-	British Museum 95 3-13 28	*Spearheads*, fig. 23b.
Croydon Surrey	grave	C1 12.3	-	-	Croydon Public Library	-
Croydon Surrey	grave	H1 14.8f	-	-	Croydon Public Library	-
Croydon Surrey	grave	C1 16.2	-	-	Croydon Public Library	-
Croydon Surrey	grave	H1 18.5(f	-	-	Croydon Public Library	-
Croydon Surrey	grave	H2 18.2f	-	-	Croydon Public Library	-
Croydon Surrey	grave	H2 21.0f	-	-	Croydon Public Library	-
Croydon Surrey	grave	H2 25.0	-	-	Croydon Public Library	-
Croydon Surrey	grave	K1 26.0	-	-	Croydon Public Library	-
Croydon Surrey	grave	E3 33.2	-	-	Croydon Public Library	-
Croydon Surrey	grave	E3 f)35.2	-	-	Croydon Public Library	-
Croydon Surrey	grave	D2 f)35.0	-	-	Croydon Public Library	-
Croydon Surrey	grave	H3 36.8	-	-	Croydon Public Library	-
Croydon Surrey	grave	C3 40.0	-	-	Croydon Public Library	-
Darenth Kent	grave	H2 21.7	-	shield	Dartford Museum	-
Darlington Durham	grave 2	E3 f31.4f	-	-	Darlington Museum	*VCH. Durham*, I, 211, pl.
Darlington Durham	grave 3	C3 39.5	-	-	Darlington Museum	*VCH. Durham*, I, 211, pl.
Dawes Heath Essex	grave	E2 f24.6	-	knife	Southend Museum 437.33	-
Dinton Bucks.	grave	E1 13.8	-	knife	-	*Nenia Britannica*, 69, pl. xvi,4.
Ditton Kent	?grave	H3 f)24.2	-	-	Maidstone Museum 49 1962	*Arch.Cantiana*, LXXVII, 1962, 204-5.
Dorchester Oxon.	grave	H2 f22.4	-	shield	British Museum 1920 11-23 2	*Guildhall Museum Catalogue*, 120-1
		L f)21.2	-		British Museum 1920 11-23 3	*Guildhall Museum Catalogue*, 120-1.
Dorchester I Oxon.	grave 1	B2 17.3f	-	knife	Ashmolean Museum 1886 1707	*Spearheads*, 215.
Dorchester III Oxon.	grave 2	L 17.2	-	-	Ashmolean Museum 1947 410	-

Provenance	Nature of find.	Type Length	Butt-ferrule	Associated weapons.	Museum Accession no.	Publication
Dorchester Oxon.	River Thames	E1 f)10.2f	-	-	Reading Museum 265.61	-
Dorking Surrey	?grave	C3 f23.7f	-	-	Guildford Museum S.6980	-
Dover B Kent	grave C	H3 52.8	conical 15.0	knife, sword, shield	British Museum 1963 11-8 747	*Archaeologia*, CI, 1967, 86, fig. 4.
Dover B Kent	grave 4	E3 f28.3	-	knife	British Museum 1963 11-8 17	-
Dover B Kent	grave 8	D2 f31.4(f	-	knife	British Museum 1963 11-8 39	-
Dover B Kent	grave 9	E2 f17.5	-	knife	British Museum 1963 11-8 42	-
Dover B Kent	grave 10	E3 f)37.8	-	knife	British Museum 1963 11-8 46	-
Dover B Kent	grave 27	D1 27.8	* 6.0	knife, sword, shield	British Museum 1963 11-8 129-30	-
Dover B Kent	grave 33	G2 f)47.2	-	knife, sword	British Museum 1963 11-8 173	*Spearheads*, 189, fig, 35d.
Dover B Kent	grave 39	E4 f)36.3	-	knife, sword	British Museum 1963 11-8 270	-
Dover B Kent	grave 41	D1 22.9	* 5.5	knife, sword	British Museum 1963 11-8 275	-
Dover B Kent	grave 50	D2 36.6	-	knife	British Museum 1963 11-8 310	*Spearheads*, 173, fig, 20b,
Dover B Kent	grave 56	E3 46.3	-	knife, sword shield	British Museum 1963 11-8 342	*Spearheads*, 179.
Dover B Kent	grave 57	E4 f)27.7	-	knife	British Museum 1963 11-8 351	-
Dover B Kent	grave 61	D2 30.6	-	knife	British Museum 1963 11-8 386	-
Dover B Kent	grave 63	D2 f)33.4	-	knife	British Museum 1963 11-8 394	-
Dover B Kent	grave 65	E3 45.0	conical 7.1	knife, seax	British Museum 1963 11-8 399	-
Dover B Kent	grave 71	E3 f36.7	-	knife, sword, shield	British Museum 1963 11-8 417	-
Dover B Kent	grave 87	F1 f)19.3	conical	knife	British Museum 1963 11-8 456	*Spearheads*, 183, fig. 72a,
Dover B Kent	grave 90	D3 f15.9	-	knife, shield	British Museum 1963 11-8 460	-
Dover B Kent	grave 91	E3 41.5	conical 11.5	knife, sword, shield	British Museum 1963 11-8 468	-
Dover B Kent	grave 96a	D2 f27.8	-	knife, sword, shield	British Museum 1963 11-8 499	*Spearheads*, 173, fig. 66f,
Dover B Kent	grave 96b	D2 41.0	-	knife, sword	British Museum 1963 11-8 506	*Spearheads*, 173, fig. 661.
Dover B Kent	grave 114	C5 18.5	-	knife	British Museum 1963 11-8 562	*Spearheads*, fig. 16d.
Dover B Kent	grave 128	D2 f)24.8	-	knife	British Museum 1963 11-8 588	*Spearheads*, 173, fig. 72a.
Dover B Kent	grave 131	C3 28.5f	-	knife, sword, shield	British Museum 1963 11-8 602	-
Dover B Kent	grave 135	C5 25.7	-	knife	British Museum 1963 11-8 602	*Spearheads*, 167.
Dover B Kent	grave 137	D1 14.4	square spike 9.7	2 knives	British Museum 1963 11-8 636, 639	*Spearheads*, 169-71.
Dover B Kent	grave 156	D1 23.5	-	knife, arrows	British Museum 1963 11-8 697	*Spearheads*, 171, fig. 18b.
Dover B Kent	surface find	E4 f16.3(f	-	-	British Museum 1963 11-8 768	-
Dover B Kent	-	C2 f28.8	-	-	British Museum 1963 11-8 781	-
Driffield I Yorks.	grave 2	H3 45.5	conical 14.0	knife, shield	Hull Museum	*Forty Years' Researches*, 277, figs. 746-7.
Driffield I Yorks.	grave 5	imported 40.5	conical 16.5	knife, shield	Hull Museum	*Forty Years' Researches*, 277, fig. 759.

Provenance	Nature of find.	Type Length	Butt-ferrule	Associated weapons.	Museum Accession no.	Publication
Driffield I Yorks.	grave 6	G2 f29.0	-	knife, shield	Hull Museum	*Forty Years' Researches*, 278, fig. 767.
Driffield I Yorks.	grave 17	C3 34.0	-	knife	-	*Forty Years' Researches*, 279, fig. 780.
Driffield I Yorks.	grave 19	C1 14.4	-	knife	-	*Forty Years' Researches*, 280, fig. 791.
Driffield I Yorks.	grave 20	D1 22.2	-	knife	-	*Forty Years' Researches*, 280, fig. 792.
Driffield I Yorks.	grave	E3 f)29.0	-	-	Hull Museum	*Forty Years' Researches*, 271.
Driffield II Yorks.	grave 1	H3 34.8	conical 11.2	knife	York Museum 408-9.47	*Forty Years' Researches*, 287, fig. 838.
		D1 20.0	-		York Museum 411.47	*Forty Years' Researches*, 287, fig.
Driffield II Yorks.	grave	E3 54.3	-	-	York Museum 412.47	*Forty Years' Researches*, 287, fig. 839.
Driffield II Yorks.	grave	F3 14.1	-	-	York Museum 415.47	*Forty Years' Researches*, 286, fig. 840.
Droxford Hants.	grave	I1 29.9	-	-	British Museum 1902 7-22 90	*Spearheads*, fig. 45c.
Droxford Hants.	grave	I1 f28.4	-	-	British Museum 1902 7-22 91	-
Droxford Hants.	grave	L f24.8	-	-	British Museum 1902 7-22 92	-
Droxford Hants.	grave	K1 40.9	-	-	British Museum 1902 7-22 93	-
Droxford Hants.	grave	H3 31.8	-	-	British Museum 1902 7-22 94	-
Droxford Hants.	grave	L f)33.0	-	-	British Museum 1902 7-22 95	-
Droxford Hants.	grave	L f22.1f	-	-	British Museum 1902 7-22 96	-
Droxford Hants.	grave	H1 20.0	-	-	British Museum 1902 7-22 97	-
Droxford Hants.	grave	H2 21.2	-	-	British Museum 1902 7-22 98	-
Droxford Hants.	grave	H3 33.2	-	-	British Museum 1902 7-22 99	-
Droxford Hants.	grave	H3 28.2	-	-	British Museum 1902 7-22 100	-
Droxford Hants.	grave	H2 21.3	-	-	British Museum 1902 7-22 101	-
Droxford Hants.	grave	L f17.3f	-	-	British Museum 1902 7-22 102	-
Droxford Hants.	grave	H1 16.6	-	-	British Museum 1902 7-22 103	-
Droxford Hants.	grave	C3 34.6	-	-	British Museum 1902 7-22 104	-
Droxford Hants.	grave	D2 29.0	-	-	British Museum 1902 7-22 105	*Spearheads*, fig. 18d.
Droxford Hants.	grave	L 22.5	-	-	British Museum 1902 7-22 106	-
Droxford Hants.	grave	E1 19.2	-	-	British Museum 1902 7-22 107	*Spearheads*, fig. 23f.
Droxford Hants.	grave	H2 18.5(f	-	-	British Museum 1902 7-22 108	-
Droxford Hants.	grave	E1 18.1	-	-	British Museum 1902 7-22 109	*Spearheads*, fig. 23g.
Droxford Hants.	grave	E1 17.3	-	-	British Museum 1902 7-22 110	-
Droxford Hants.	grave	E1 14.0	-	-	British Museum 1902 7-22 111	-
Droxford Hants.	grave	E1 15.0	-	-	British Museum 1902 7-22 112	-
Droxford Hants.	grave	E1 f)13.5(f	-	-	British Museum 1902 7-22 113	-

Provenance	Nature of find.	Type Length	Butt-ferrule	Associated weapons.	Museum Accession no.	Publication
Droxford Hants.	grave	E1 f12.6(f	-	-	British Museum 1902 7-22 114	-
Droxford Hants.	grave	H1 f11.1f	-	-	British Museum 1902 7-22 115	-
Droxford Hants.	grave	D1 17.4	-	-	British Museum 1902 7-22 116	*Spearheads*, fig. 18e.
Droxford Hants.	grave	D2 17.8f	-	-	British Museum 1902 7-22 117	-
Droxford Hants.	grave	L 17.0f	-	-	British Museum 1902 7-22 118	-
Droxford Hants.	grave	J 31.2(f	-	-	British Museum 1902 7-22 119	*Spearheads*, fig. 48e.
Droxford Hants.	grave	E3 53.4	-	-	British Museum 1902 7-22 143	-
Droxford Hants.	grave	H1 17.3	-	-	British Museum 1902 7-22 144	*Spearheads*, fig. 37c.
Droxford Hants.	grave	E2 f14.7f	-	-	British Museum 1902 7-22 145	-
Droxford Hants.	grave	F1 20.1	-	-	Winchester Museum	
Duston Northants.	grave	E1 f)18.7	-	-	Northampton Museum D.377	-
Duston Northants.	grave	E4 f)27.5	-	-	Northampton Museum D.378	-
Duston Northants.	grave	E2 28.1	-	-	Northampton Museum D.379	-
Duston Northants.	grave	E4 f21.8	-	-	Northampton Museum D.380	-
Duston Northants.	grave	E2 f19.8f	-	-	Northampton Museum D.381	-
Duston Northants.	grave	H2 f25.7f	-	-	Northampton Museum D.382	-
Duston Northants.	grave	H3 f)36.8	-	-	Northampton Museum D.385	-
Duston Northants.	grave	E3 54.4	-	-	Northampton Museum D.386	-
Duston Northants.	grave	H3 38.4	-	-	Northampton Museum D.387	-
Duston Northants.	grave	E1 f)17.9	-	-	Northampton Museum D.388	-
Duston Northants.	grave	E2 f19.2	-	-	Northampton Museum D.389	-
Duston Northants.	grave	E2 f)20.4f	-	-	Northampton Museum D.390	-
Duston Northants.	grave	E1 23.3	-	-	Northampton Museum D.391	-
Duston Northants.	grave	F2 f21.4	-	-	Northampton Museum D.394	-
Duston Northants.	grave	E2 f23.1f	-	-	Northampton Museum D.395	-
Duston Northants.	grave	H2 f)22.2	-	-	Northampton Museum D.396	-
Duston Northants.	grave	H2 24.2	-	-	Northampton Museum D.397	-
Duston Northants.	grave	E2 f22.5	-	-	Northampton Museum D.398	-
Duston Northants.	grave	H2 f18.2	-	-	Northampton Museum D.399	-
Duston Northants.	grave	F2 f16.1	-	-	Northampton Museum D.400	-
Duston Northants.	grave	E2 18.8	-	-	Northampton Museum D.401	-
Duston Northants.	grave	H3 f23.9f	-	-	Northampton Museum D.402	-
Eastbourne Sussex	grave	F2 33.5	-	shield	-	*Sussex Notes & Queries*, II, 1929, 193.

Provenance	Nature of find.	Type Length	Butt-ferrule	Associated weapons.	Museum Accession no.	Publication
Eastburn Yorks.	grave	B2 f11.5	-	-	-	*Yorks.Arch.Journal*, XXXIV, 1938-9, 40, pl. i,2.
East Ewell Surrey	grave	C4 42.1	-	knife, shield	Guildford Museum RB.1274	*Antiqu.Journal*, XLIII, 1963, 294-6, pl.1, fig. 1c.
East Grafton Wilts.	grave	G2 31.3f	-	-	Newbury Museum	*Wilts.Arch.Magazine*, XLVI, 1934, 164.
East Kent	-	F3 f22.6(f	-	-	Liverpool Museum	-
East Kent	-	C2 22.7	-	-	Liverpool Museum	-
East Kent	-	E4 f22.4(f	-	-	Liverpool Museum	-
East Kent	-	E3 f)28.8f	-	-	Liverpool Museum	-
East Kent	-	H3 f24.1(f	-	-	Liverpool Museum	-
East Kent	-	H2 21.0	-	-	Liverpool Museum	-
East Kent	-	C3 25.3	-	-	Liverpool Museum	-
East Kent	-	E2 f16.7f	-	-	Liverpool Museum	-
East Kent	-	G2 f14.6f	-	-	Liverpool Museum	-
East Kent	-	C2 f)25.2	-	-	Liverpool Museum	-
East Kent	-	C2 f23.1f	-	-	Liverpool Museum	-
East Kent	-	E3 f)39.4	-	-	Liverpool Museum	-
East Kent	-	H3 31.9(f	-	-	Liverpool Museum	-
East Kent	-	H3 f29.9	-	-	Liverpool Museum	-
East Kent	-	E2 f25.8	-	-	Liverpool Museum	-
East Kent	-	C1 f)18.6	-	-	Liverpool Museum	-
East Kent	-	E4 f25.9(f	-	-	Liverpool Museum	-
East Kent	-	D2 f15.3f	-	-	Liverpool Museum	-
East Kent	-	D1 23.0	-	-	Liverpool Museum	-
East Kent	-	E3 f31.6f	-	-	Liverpool Museum	-
East Kent	-	E2 19.6	-	-	Liverpool Museum	-
East Kent	-	H3 33.1f	-	-	Liverpool Museum	-
East Kent	-	E4 f)38.7	-	-	Liverpool Museum	-
East Kent	-	E3 f)39.4	-	-	Liverpool Museum	-
East Kent	-	E3 f)36.8	-	-	Liverpool Museum	-
East Kent	-	D2 f)32.6	-	-	Liverpool Museum	-
East Kent	-	D2 f)30.1(f	-	-	Liverpool Museum	-
East Kent	-	C3 f32.3	-	-	Liverpool Museum	-
East Kent	-	H3 f25.6	-	-	Liverpool Museum	-
East Kent	-	C2 28.2	-	-	Liverpool Museum	-

Provenance	Nature of find.	Type Length	Butt-ferrule	Associated weapons.	Museum Accession no.	Publication
East Kent	-	G2 f21.8f	-	-	Liverpool Museum	-
East Kent	-	E2 f15.6f	-	-	Liverpool Museum	-
East Kent	-	D2 26.3f	-	-	Liverpool Museum	-
East Kent	-	D2 f20.8	-	-	Liverpool Museum	-
East Kent	-	H3 f26.5f	-	-	Liverpool Museum	-
East Kent	-	C2 f32.1	-	-	Liverpool Museum	-
East Kent	-	E3 f31.7	-	-	Liverpool Museum	-
East Kent	-	E3 f43.7f	-	-	Liverpool Museum	-
East Kent	-	E3 f)38.1(f	-	-	Liverpool Museum	-
East Kent	-	E3 52.0	-	-	Liverpool Museum	-
East Kent	-	H3 f)45.0	-	-	Liverpool Museum	-
East Kent	-	C2 f)18.8f	-	-	Liverpool Museum	-
East Kent	-	C3 22.5f	-	-	Liverpool Museum	-
East Kent	-	C1 f)18.9	-	-	Liverpool Museum	-
East Kent	-	E3 f)34.0	-	-	Liverpool Museum	-
East Kent	-	H3 31.4	-	-	Liverpool Museum	-
East Kent	-	C5 19.4f	-	-	Liverpool Museum	-
East Kent	-	B2 f14.5	-	-	Liverpool Museum	-
East Kent	-	D2 f)28.6	-	-	Liverpool Museum	-
East Kent	-	D1 30.2	-	-	Liverpool Museum	-
East Kent	-	D2 f)24.9f	-	-	Liverpool Museum	-
East Kent	-	F3 27.3	-	-	Liverpool Museum	-
East Kent	-	H3 f)38.6	-	-	Liverpool Museum	-
East Kent	-	E3 f)38.4	-	-	Liverpool Museum	-
East Kent	-	E3 f)35.2f	-	-	Liverpool Museum	-
East Kent	-	C4 f)37.9f	-	-	Liverpool Museum	-
East Shefford Berks.	grave 2	H1 f)17.8	-	-	Newbury Museum	J.Royal Anthropol.Inst., XLV, 1915, 120.
East Shefford Berks.	grave	L 29.5	-	-	Ashmolean Museum 1955 351	-
East Shefford Berks.	grave	H2 f)22.9	-	-	Ashmolean Museum 1955 352	-
East Shefford Berks.	grave	K1 21.0	-	-	Ashmolean Museum 1955 353	-
East Shefford Berks.	grave	E1 20.3	-	-	Ashmoelan Museum 1955 354	-
East Shefford Berks.	grave 39	H1 21.9	-	2 knives	British Museum 93 7-16 117	-
East Shefford Berks.	grave	H2 22.3	-	-	British Museum 93 7-16 130	-

Provenance	Nature of find.	Type Length	Butt-ferrule	Associated weapons.	Museum Accession no.	Publication
East Shefford Berks.	grave	H1 18.1	-	-	British Museum 93 7-16 131	-
East Shefford Berks.	grave	G1 28.8	-	-	British Museum 93 7-16 132	Proc.Newbury Field Club, IV, 1896, 196.
East Shefford Berks.	grave 48	C1 16.4	-	-	British Museum 93 7-16 133	Spearheads, fig. 9c.
East Shefford Berks.	grave	H2 22.4	-	-	British Museum	-
East Shefford Berks.	grave	C4 f45.7f	-	-	British Museum	-
East Shefford Berks.	grave	E1 f)17.1	-	-	British Museum	-
East Shefford Berks.	grave	H3 f)23.3f	-	-	British Museum	-
Emscote Warwicks.	grave	L f)35.6	-	-	British Museum 1925 6-8 13	-
Emscote Warwicks.	grave	H3 30.3	-	-	British Museum 1925 6-8 14	-
Emscote Warwicks.	grave	E2 21.2	-	-	British Museum 1925 6-8 15	-
Esher Surrey	grave A	E3 f)31.5f	-	shield	-	Antiqu.Journal, XXVII, 1947, 35, fig. 15.
Ewell Surrey	grave	F1 17.2f	-	-	Guildford Museum	Antiqu.Journal, XII, 1932, 444, fig. 3,2.
Ewell Surrey	grave	H3 33.2	-	-	Guildford Museum	Antiqu.Journal, XII, 1932, 444, fig. 3,1.
Ewell Surrey	grave	H2 20.0	-	shield	London Museum 32.176.1	Antiqu.Journal, XII, 1932, 444, fig. 3,3.
Ewell Surrey	grave	H1 18.5	-	shield	London Museum 32.176.2	Antiqu.Journal, XII, 1932, 444, fig. 3,4.
Exning Suffolk	grave	G2 f)33.6	-	-	Cambridge Museum A.1904 438	Cambridge Region, 264, pl. 36.
Exning Suffolk	grave	E2 27.4	conical 7.4	-	Cambridge Museum A.1904 439	Cambridge Region, 264, pl. 36.
Eynsham Oxon.	grave	K1 19.9	-	knife, shield	Ashmolean Museum 1952 399	-
Eythrope Bucks.	-	C2 32.4f	-	-	Aylesbury Museum 43.05	-
Fairford Glos.	grave 2	H2 f)23.5	-	shield	Ashmolean Museum 1961 3	Fairford Graves, 13, fig. 11,3.
Fairford Glos.	grave 2	B2 41.1	•	shield	Ashmolean Museum 1961 4	Fairford Graves, 13, fig. 11,2.
Fairford Glos.	graves 8-12	C1 18.3(f	-	-	Ashmolean Museum 1961 28	Fairford Graves, 19, fig. 11,5.
Fairford Glos.	graves 8-12	C1 13.8	-	-	Ashmolean Museum 1961 29	Fairford Graves, 19, fig. 11,6.
Fairford Glos.	grave 13	L f)25.5	-	shield	Ashmolean Museum 1961 31	Fairford Graves, 19, fig. 11,2.
Fairford Glos.	grave 23	H1 17.4	-	knife, shield	Ashmolean Museum 1961 38	Fairford Graves, 19, fig. 11,7.
Fairford Glos.	grave 28	K1 25.7	conical 9.5	knife, shield	Ashmolean Museum 1961 45-7	Fairford Graves, 20, fig. 11,4,8.
Fairford Glos.	grave 45	C2 27.8	-	knife	Ashmolean Museum 1961 59	Fairford Graves, 29, fig. 11,1.
Fairford Glos.	grave	C1 f)13.5	-	-	Ashmolean Museum 1851 142	Spearheads, fig. 9d.
Fairford Glos.	grave	K2 26.4	-	-	Ashmolean Museum 1961 59	-
Fairford Glos.	grave	C1 14.4	-	-	Ashmolean Museum 1961 75	-
Fairford Glos.	grave	L 22.2	conical 8.2	-	Ashmolean Museum 1961 76,78	-
Fairford Glos.	grave	L f)22.1	conical 5.2	-	Ashmolean Museum 1961 77,79	-
Fairford Glos.	grave	H1 17.3	-	-	Ashmolean Museum 1961 88	-

Provenance	Nature of find.	Type Length	Butt-ferrule	Associated weapons	Museum Accession no.	Publication
Fairford Glos.	grave	H3 f24.0	-	-	Gloucester Museum A.3660	-
Fairford Glos.	grave	L 22.2	-	-	Gloucester Museum A.3661	*Spearheads*, fig. 53c.
Fareham II Hants.	grave	H3 f)32.9	-	-	Winchester Museum	-
Farningham Kent	grave	C2 f)20.8(f	-	knife	Dartford Museum	-
Farningham Kent	grave	C2 f)28.4(f	-	knife, seax, shield	Dartford Museum	*Spearheads*, 157.
Farthingdown Surrey	grave	E2 f26.4	-	-	Guildford Museum S.6991	-
Farthingdown Surrey	grave	E3 f)50.0	-	-	Ashmolean Museum 1885 144	-
Farthingdown Surrey	grave	C3 34.2	-	-	Ashmolean Museum 1885 145	-
Farthingdown Surrey	grave	C2 26.2	-	-	Ashmolean Museum 1885 147	-
Farthingdown Surrey	grave	C2 21.5	-	-	Ashmolean Museum 1885 148	-
Faversham II Kent	grave	H3 39.5	-	-	British Museum 83 12-13 654	-
Faversham II Kent	grave	H3 f30.5f	-	-	British Museum 83 12-13 655	-
Faversham II Kent	grave	F1 f)16.4f	-	-	British Museum 83 12-13 657	-
Faversham II Kent	grave	E2 f13.0f	-	-	British Museum 83 12-13 659	-
Faversham II Kent	grave	E2 f)18.8f	-	-	British Museum 83 12-13 661	-
Faversham II Kent	grave	E4 f22.4f	-	-	British Museum 891.70	-
Faversham II Kent	grave	G2 f23.3f	-	-	British Museum 973.70	-
Faversham II Kent	grave	E3 f28.9f	-	-	British Museum 975.70	-
Faversham II Kent	grave	H3 f25.5f	-	-	British Museum 977.70	-
Faversham II Kent	grave	E3 f24.4	-	-	British Museum 979.70	-
Faversham II Kent	grave	D2 f)23.3f	-	-	British Museum 980.70	-
Faversham II Kent	grave	E2 f)28.6	-	-	British Museum 984.70	-
Faversham II Kent	grave	E2 f22.4f	-	-	British Museum 985.70	-
Faversham II Kent	grave	E3 f24.6	-	-	British Museum 986.70	-
Faversham II Kent	grave	G2 f27.5f	-	-	British Museum 987.70	-
Faversham II Kent	grave	E2 f12.4f	-	-	British Museum 989.70	-
Faversham II Kent	grave	E2 f)16.1f	-	-	British Museum 991.70	-
Faversham II Kent	grave	F1 f)13.4f	-	-	British Museum 993.70	-
Faversham II Kent	grave	H3 f22.3f	-	-	British Museum 994.70	-
Faversham II Kent	grave	H3 40.2	-	-	British Museum	-
Faversham II Kent	grave	H3 f33.3f	-	-	British Museum	-
Faversham II Kent	grave	H3 f)34.2f	-	-	British Museum	-
Faversham II Kent	grave	E3 18.9f	-	-	British Museum	-

Provenance	Nature of find.	Type Length	Butt-ferrule	Associated weapons.	Museum Accession no.	Publication
Faversham II Kent	grave	C2 21.1f	-	-	British Museum	-
Faversham II Kent	grave	E3 f)38.6f	-	-	Farnham Museum 1024	-
Feering Essex	grave	H2 27.2	-	knife, sword	Colchester Museum 170	-
Feering Essex	grave	C2 21.3	-	-	Colchester Museum 170.95	-
Feering Essex	grave	F1 f)17.3	-	-	Colchester Museum 564.28	-
Fen Ditton Cambs.	grave	L f)20.9	-	-	Cambridge Museum 58.152	-
Fen Ditton Cambs.	grave	H3 f)31.9	-	-	Cambridge Museum 58.152	-
Fen Ditton Cambs.	grave	C2 30.8	-	-	Cambridge Museum 58.152	-
Fen Ditton Cambs.	grave	G1 14.7f	-	-	Cambridge Museum 58.152	-
Fetcham Surrey	grave	C4 f.34.8	-	-	Guildford Museum S.5944	-
Fetcham Surrey	grave	E4 30.9(f	-	-	Guildford Museum S.5945	-
Fetcham Surrey	grave	E3 f)32.7	-	-	Guildford Museum S.5946	-
Fetcham Surrey	grave	H2 f)25.8	-	-	Guildford Museum S.5947	-
Fetcham Surrey	grave	L f)22.2	-	-	Guildford Museum S.5948	-
Fetcham Surrey	grave	H1 f)12.9f	-	-	Guildford Museum S.5951	-
Figheldean Wilts.	grave	H1 17.2	-	-	Salisbury Museum 122.37	Wilts.Arch.Magazine, XXXVIII, 1913, 254.
Finglesham Kent	grave G2	F3e 36.0	conical 14.0	2 knives, sword,	Deal Castle Museum	Medieval Archaeology, II, 1958, 22, fig.14b.
Finglesham Kent	grave G6	E2 f)22.4f	-	knife, ?shield	Deal Castle Museum	Medieval Archaeology, II, 1958, 25, fig.15b.
Finglesham Kent	grave H3	D1 f)26.5	-	knife, seax	Deal Castle Museum	Medieval Archaeology, II, 1958, 25, pl.15a.
Finglesham Kent	grave 6	C2 f25.0	-	knife	-	Spearheads, 157.
Finglesham Kent	grave 74	B1 14.5	-	knife	-	-
Finglesham Kent	grave 82	C5 25.6	-	knife	-	Spearheads, 167.
Finglesham Kent	grave 83	C5 22.8	band diam. 3.5	seax	-	Spearheads, 167.
Finglesham Kent	grave 86	D2 f21.5f	-	knife	-	Spearheads, 173.
Finglesham Kent	grave 95	F1 22.4	-	knife	-	Spearheads, 183.
Finglesham Kent	grave 102	E3 45.0	-	knife	-	-
Finglesham Kent	grave 103	F2 25.6	-	knife	-	-
Finglesham Kent	grave 107	E2 f34.4	-	-	-	-
Finglesham Kent	grave 117	B2 30.5	band with spike diam. 2.0	knife	-	-
Finglesham Kent	grave 133	C5 26.3	band with spike diam. 2.0	knife	-	Spearheads, 167-9, fig. 64d.
Finglesham Kent	grave 135	D2 29.0	-	knife	-	-
Finglesham Kent	grave 143	B1 10.2	-	-	-	-
Finglesham Kent	grave 144	C5 15.4	-	knife	-	-

Provenance	Nature of find	Type Length	Butt-ferrule	Associated weapons	Museum Accession no.	Publication
Finglesham Kent	grave 159	C3 52.4	-	knife	-	*Spearheads*, 163.
Finglesham Kent	grave 170	C5 19.5	-	knife	-	-
Finglesham Kent	grave 181	D1 f)29.0	-	knife	-	*Spearheads*, 171.
Finglesham Kent	grave 198	E2 f)41.2	-	knife	-	-
Finglesham Kent	grave 204	K1 25.5	conical 8.5	knife, sword, shield	-	*Spearheads*, 209.
Finglesham Kent	grave 211	F1 f)18.8	conical 12.5	shield	-	-
Folkestone III Kent	grave 5	G2 58.2	-	shield	Folkestone Museum	*Spearheads*, fig. 35e.
Folkestone III Kent	grave 7	G2 27.7f	conical 7.0	knife	Folkestone Museum	-
Folkestone III Kent	grave 10	D2 f)35.0(f	-	knife, sword	Folkestone Museum	-
Folkestone III Kent	grave 11	E4 43.2	-	knife	Folkestone Museum	-
Folkestone III Kent	grave 15	G1 f20.1	-	larger and smaller knives	Folkestone Museum	-
Folkestone III Kent	grave 18	E3 f)36.1	-	knife, shield, another spear	Folkestone Museum	-
Folkestone III Kent	grave	F1 9.1	-	-	Folkestone Museum	-
Folkestone III Kent	grave	E4 40.6	-	-	Folkestone Museum	-
Folkestone III Kent	grave	F1 f)10.0f	-	-	Folkestone Museum	-
Folkestone III Kent	grave	E3 27.8f	-	-	Folkestone Museum	-
Folkestone III Kent	grave	E3 42.2	-	-	Folkestone Museum	-
Fonaby Lincs.	grave 24	H1 21.1	-	2 knives, shield	Scunthorpe Museum	*Spearheads*, 193, fig. 77c.
		H2 25.3f	conical 6.9		Scunthorpe Museum	*Spearheads*, 193, 196.
Ford Wilts.	grave	C3 38.0	-	seax, shield	Salisbury Museum 18.64	*Antiqu.Journal*, XLIX, 1969, 104, fig.5.
		C3 37.2	-		Salisbury Museum 18.64	*Antiqu.Journal*, XLIX, 1969, 104, fig.5.
Fordham Cambs.	-	H1 f19.7	-	-	Cambridge Museum 1903 166	-
Fordwells Oxon.	-	C2 f)18.2	-	-	Bristol Museum F.2231	-
Fornham Suffolk	grave	E1 15.8	-	-	Bury St Edmunds Museum K.47	-
Fornham Suffolk	grave	E1 f8.9f	-	-	Bury St Edmunds Museum K.47	-
Fornham Suffolk	grave	E1 14.6	-	-	Bury St Edmunds Museum K.47	*Spearheads*, fig. 23a.
Foxhill Wilts.	grave	H2 20.7	-	-	Devizes Museum 9	*Wilts.Arch.Magazine*, XLIX, 1942, 542.
Frilford I Berks.	grave 4	E1 16.0	-	shield	Ashmolean Museum 1886 1436	*Archaeologia*, XLII, 1869, 469, pl.xxiii,6.
Frilford I Berks.	grave	L 27.0	-	knife, shield	-	*Archaeologia*, XLII, 1869, 474, pl.xxiii,7.
Frilford I Berks.	grave	J f)29.3	-	-	Ashmolean Museum 1868	-
Frilford I Berks.	grave	F1 20.5	-	-	Ashmolean Museum 1868 1437	-
Frilford I Berks.	grave	L f)22.8	-	-	Ashmolean Museum 1873 1422	-
Frilford I Berks.	grave	H3 30.1	-	shield	Ashmolean Museum 1886 1425	-

Provenance	Nature of find.	Type Length	Butt-ferrule	Associated weapons.	Museum Accession no.	Publication
Frilford I Berks.	grave	C1 12.7	-	-	Ashmolean Museum 1892 2634	-
Frilford I Berks.	grave	K1 f)20.1	-	-	Ashmolean Museum 1892 2635	*Spearheads*, fig. 50b.
Frilford I Berks.	grave	B2 f)25.0	-	-	Ashmolean Museum 1892 2637	-
Frilford I Berks.	grave	C2 f)25.6f	-	-	Ashmolean Museum 1892 2638	-
Friskney Lincs.	grave	H2 f)21.5	-	-	Farnham Museum 1382	-
Friskney Lincs.	grave	C2 20.7f	-	-	Farnham Museum	-
Friskney Lincs.	grave	H2 25.5	-	-	Farnham Museum	-
Friskney Lincs.	grave	E4 30.9f	-	-	Farnham Museum	-
Garrowby Wold Yorks.	grave B69	E3 f)29.0	-	-	Hull Museum	*Forty Years' Researches*, 144, fig. 387.
Garton I Yorks	grave	C1 13.5	-	4 other spears	Hull Museum	*Forty Years' Researches*, 237, fig. 599.
		C1 f13.0	-		Hull Museum	*Forty Years' Researches*, 237, fig. 600.
		C1 16.5	-		Hull Museum	*Forty Years' Researches*, 237, fig. 600.
Garton Slack I Yorks.	grave	C1 19.0f	-	-	-	*Forty Years' Researches*, 268, fig. 733.
Gilton Kent	grave A	G1 28.0	-	shield	-	*Nenia Britannica*, 27, pl. vii,3.
Gilton Kent	grave 1	E3 45.5	-	knife	-	*Inventorium Sepulchrale*, 4, fig. 14.
Gilton Kent	grave 4	C1 7.5	-	-	-	*Inventorium Sepulchrale*, 4, fig. 10.
Gilton Kent	grave 5	E3 c45.0	-	knife, shield	-	*Faussett Papers*.
		D1 c22.0	-		-	*Inventorium Sepulchrale*, 5, fig. 10; *F.Papers*.
Gilton Kent	grave 6	E3	-	knife, shield	-	*Faussett Papers*.
Gilton Kent	grave 7	D1	-	knife	-	*Inventorium Sepulchrale*, 6.
Gilton Kent	grave 10	C3 50.0	cylindrical	knife, sword, seax, shield	-	*Inventorium Sepulchrale*, 7, fig.
Gilton Kent	grave 23	E3	-	2 knives, sword, shield	-	*Inventorium Sepulchrale*, 11.
		E3	-		-	*Inventorium Sepulchrale*, 11.
Gilton Kent	grave 28	E3 c44.4	conical	-	-	*Faussett Papers*.
Gilton Kent	grave 46	C1	-	2 knives	-	*Inventorium Sepulchrale*, 17, fig. 10.
		C1	-		-	*Inventorium Sepulchrale*, 17, fig. 10.
Gilton Kent	grave 48	E3 c45.0	-	2 knives, sword, shield	-	*Inventorium Sepulchrale*, 17.
Gilton Kent	grave 80	C1	-	2 knives	-	*Inventorium Sepulchrale*, 25.
Gilton Kent	grave 89	E3	-	sword, shield	-	*Inventorium Sepulchrale*, 29.
Gilton Kent	grave	E3 29.4f	-	-	Liverpool Museum 6375.1	-
Gilton Kent	grave	C4 f)46.3	-	-	Liverpool Museum	-
Girton Cambs.	grave	F1 f13.9	-	-	Cambridge Museum 240	-
Girton Cambs.	grave	E2 29.2	-	-	Cambridge Museum 24.11	-

Provenance	Nature of find.	Type Length	Butt-ferrule	Associated weapons.	Museum Accession no.	Publication
Glen Parva Leics.	grave	I2 f)28.9	-	sword	Leicester Museum 51 1880	Spearheads, fig. 47d.
Gloucester Glos.	-	C2 16.5f	-	-	Gloucester Museum A.2681	-
Gt Chesterford Essex	grave A	B2 35.0	-	2 knives	-	Arch.Journal, XIII, 1856, 2, pl.i,12.
Gt Chesterford Essex	grave 2	H2 24.1	-	knife	British Museum 1964 7-2 14	Spearheads, 196.
Gt Chesterford Essex	grave 4	H2 24.7	-	shield	British Museum 1964 7-2 28	-
Gt Chesterford Essex	grave 16	H1 18.0	-	knife, shield	British Museum 1964 7-2 68	Spearheads, 193.
Gt Chesterford Essex	grave 19	L 31.6	-	-	British Museum 1964 7-2 95	-
Gt Chesterford Essex	grave 22	H1 18.1 / H1 20.7	conical 7.3 / conical 7.7	knife, shield	British Museum 1964 7-2 113,115 / British Museum 1964 7-2 114,116	-
Gt Chesterford Essex	grave 50	L 20.5	-	-	British Museum 1964 7-2 201	-
Gt Chesterford Essex	grave 51	H3 44.2	-	knife	British Museum 1964 7-2 491	Antiqu.Journal, XXXV, 1955, 20, pl. 3c.
Gt Chesterford Essex	grave 76	F2 19.4	-	shield	British Museum 1964 7-2 266	-
Gt Chesterford Essex	grave 86	H1 17.7	-	knife, shield	British Museum 1964 7-2 284	-
Gt Chesterford Essex	grave 96	H2 27.4	conical 10.4	knife	British Museum 1964 7-2 299,300	-
Gt Chesterford Essex	grave 99	H2 20.0	-	knife	British Museum 1964 7-2 308	-
Gt Chesterford Essex	grave 101	C3 35.4	-	knife	British Museum 1964 7-2 318	-
Gt Chesterford Essex	grave 115	L 24.0	conical 3.9	knife	British Museum 1964 7-2 347,348	Spearheads, 215, fig.88d.
Gt Chesterford Essex	grave 157	J 28.5	-	knife	British Museum 1964 7-2 436	Spearheads, 209, fig.85g.
Gt Tosson Northumberland	grave	C2 16.0	-	-	-	PSAS., IV, 1863, 58, fig.
Gt Wakering Essex	grave	C3 f28.0f	conical	-	British Museum 92 11-4 17,18	-
Gt Wakering Essex	grave	C1 f)17.8	-	-	Southend Museum 230.17	-
Greenwich Park London	grave	H3 38.0	-	knife, shield	-	Nenia Britannica, 90.
Greetwell Lincs.	surface	L f42.5	-	-	Lincoln Museum 97.57	Antiqu.Journal, XXXVIII, 1958, 240.
Guildown Surrey	grave 56	B2 34.1	conical 20.9	-	Guildford Museum S.3121-2	Surrey Arch.Collections, XXXIX, 1931, 13, pl. x,1.
Guildown Surrey	grave 111	I1 26.8	-	-	Guildford Museum S.3123	Surrey Arch.Collections, XXXIX, 1931, 13-4, pl. x,2.
Guildown Surrey	grave 136	C2 21.2	-	knife	Guildford Museum S.3129	Surrey Arch.Collections, XXXIX, 1931, 14-5, pl. x,3.
Guildown Surrey	grave 138	C1 8.2	*	-	-	Surrey Arch.Collections, XXXIX, 1931, 15, pl. x,4.
Guildown Surrey	grave 223	B2 f19.8	-	knife	Guildford Museum S.3126	Surrey Arch.Collections, XXXIX, 1931, 15.
Hammersmith London	River Thames	E3 39.5	-	-	Gunnersbury Park Museum 0.2067	-
Hammersmith London	River Thames	E4 41.5	-	-	London Museum 0.2041	-
Hammersmith London	River Thames	E4 f)39.8	-	-	London Museum 0.2066	-
Hampton Court Middlesex	River Thames	H1 15.6f	-	-	British Museum 1937 1-4 3	-
Ham Hill Ditch Wilts.	grave	E2 25.4	-	-	Salisbury Museum 28.61	Salisbury Museum Report, 1961, 16.

Provenance	Nature of find.	Type Length	Butt-ferrule	Associated weapons.	Museum Accession no.	Publication
Hanwell Middlesex	?grave	I1 23.2	-	-	London Museum 49.107.888	*Spearheads*, fig.45b.
Hardingstone Northants.	-	E2 27.8	-	-	Northampton Museum D.231	-
Hardingstone Northants.	-	E4 f22.3f	-	-	Northampton Museum D.233	-
Hardown Hill Dorset	grave	H2 31.0	conical 12.5	knife, ?axe, shield	Dorchester Museum 1927.6.1	*Proc.Dorset Arch.Soc.*, LIII, 1931, 248, pl.
		H1 18.7	-		Dorchester Museum 1927.6.1	*Proc.Dorset Arch.Soc.*, LIII, 1931, 248, pl.
		E1 21.1	-		Dorchester Museum 1927.6.1	*Proc.Dorset Arch.Soc.*, LIII, 1931, 248, pl.
		C2 25.6	-		Dorchester Museum 1927.6.1	*Proc.Dorset Arch.Soc.*, LIII, 1931, 248, pl.
		H1 f)19.2	-		Dorchester Museum 1927.6.1	*Proc.Dorset Arch.Soc.*, LIII, 1931, 248, pl.
		C1 14.8(f	-		Dorchester Museum 1927.6.1	*Proc.Dorset Arch.Soc.*, LIII, 1931, 248, pl.
		C1 f)19.8	-		Dorchester Museum 1927.6.1	*Proc.Dorset Arch.Soc.*, LIII, 1931, 248, pl.
		C2 f)20.5(f	-		Dorchester Museum 1927.6.1	*Proc.Dorset Arch.Soc.*, LIII, 1931, 248, pl.
Harnham Hill Wilts.	grave	L 30.5	-	-	British Museum 53 12-14 3	*Archaeologia*, XXXV, 1855, 259, pl. x,3.
Harnham Hill Wilts.	grave 1	C3 30.4	-	knife, shield	British Museum 53 12-14 5	*Archaeologia*, XXXV, 1855, 259, pl. x,4.
Harnham Hill Wilts.	grave 9	H1 16.0	-	knife	British Museum 53 12-14 7	*Archaeologia*, XXXV, 1855, 260, pl. x,5
Harnham Hill Wilts.	grave 14	J 25.1	-	-	British Museum 53 12-14 23	*Archaeologia*, XXXV, 1855, 261, pl. x,6.
Harnham Hill Wilts.	grave 17	C4 36.7	- -	knife	British Museum 53 12-14 24	*Archaeologia*, XXXV, 1855, 261.
Harnham Hill Wilts.	grave 24	H2 28.4	-	-	British Museum 53 12-14 28	*Archaeologia*, XXXV, 1855, 261.
Harwell Berks.	grave 1	B1 17.7	-	knife	Ashmolean Museum 1955 466	*Oxoniensia*, XXI, 1956, 28, fig. 10b.
Harwell Berks.	grave 7	C2 22.0	-	-	Ashmolean Museum 1966 1182	*Oxoniensia*, XXXII, 1967, 73-4, fig.14.
Haslingfield Cambs.	grave	F1 f)16.2	-	-	British Museum	-
Haslingfield Cambs.	grave	E3 f23.9	-	-	British Museum	-
Haslingfield Cambs.	grave	L f)20.3	-	-	British Museum	-
Haslingfield Cambs.	grave	H3 41.3	-	-	British Museum	-
Haslingfield Cambs.	grave	H3 41.5	-	-	British Museum	-
Haslingfield Cambs.	grave	F1 f)17.3	-	-	British Museum	-
Haslingfield Cambs.	grave	C1 f)10.5	-	-	British Museum	-
Haslingfield Cambs.	grave	F1 f)13.1	-	-	British Museum	-
Haslingfield Cambs.	grave	E1 f9.2f	-	-	British Museum	-
Haslingfield Cambs.	grave	C2 f)20.8	-	-	British Museum	-
Haslingfield Cambs.	grave	E2 19.0	-	-	British Museum	-
Haslingfield Cambs.	grave	C3 31.0f	-	-	British Museum	-
Haslingfield Cambs.	grave	H3 38.5	-	-	British Museum	-
Haslingfield Cambs.	grave	C1 16.0	-	-	British Museum	-

Provenance	Nature of find.	Type Length	Butt-ferrule	Associated weapons.	Museum Accession no.	Publication
Hassocks Sussex	grave	E3 f)36.6f	-	-	Brighton Museum 675.137-8	-
Hassocks Sussex	grave	H3 f19.6f	-	-	Brighton Museum 675.137-8	-
Heyford Purcell Oxon.	grave	H2 27.3	-	knife	Ashmolean Museum 1893 196	*Spearheads*, 155, 197.
		C1 18.9	-		Ashmolean Museum 1893 197	*Spearheads*. 155.
Hidcote Bartrim Glos.	?grave	C1 12.2	-	-	Stratford Museum	*Spearheads,* 157.
High Down Sussex	grave	A2 f)74.2(f	-	-	Worthing Museum	*Archaeologia*, LIV, 1895, 369-78, fig. 1.
High Down Sussex	grave 4	L 31.9	-	-	Worthing Museum	*Archaeologia*, LIV, 1895, 372.
High Down Sussex	grave 5	H1 18.1	-	-	Worthing Museum	*Archaeologia*, LIV, 1895, 372.
High Down Sussex	grave 14	I1 f)26.9	-	knife	Worthing Museum	*Archaeologia*, LIV, 1895, 374.
High Down Sussex	grave 20	H1 f)20.6	-	-	Worthing Museum	*Archaeologia*, LIV, 1895, 376.
High Down Sussex	grave	H3 44.1	-	-	Worthing Museum	-
High Down Sussex	grave	E3 36.4	-	-	Worthing Museum	-
High Down Sussex	grave	H1 f)16.4	-	-	Worthing Museum	-
High Down Sussex	grave	H3 25.5	-	-	Worthing Museum	-
Hinchingbrooke Hunts.	-	H3 38.5	-	-	Cambridge Museum 48.1672	*Spearheads*, fig. 41a.
Hinckley Leics.	grave	C2 31.7	-	-	Ashmolean Museum 421	-
Hinckley Leics.	grave	C1 13.1	-	-	Ashmolean Museum 422	-
Hinckley Leics.	grave	B2 f)31.5	-	shield	Ashmolean Museum	-
		H2 25.2	-		Ashmolean Museum	-
Hinton Down Wilts.	grave	E3 28.3	-	knife	Devizes Museum 52	*Wilts.Arch.Magazine*, XLIV, 1928, 244.
Holborough Kent	grave 3	E3 31.3	-	shield, another spear	Maidstone Museum	*Arch.Cantiana*, LXX, 1956, 118, fig.14,1.
Holborough Kent	grave 7	G2 39.9f	*	knife, sword shield	Maidstone Museum	*Arch.Cantiana*, LXX, 1956, 119, fig.15,1, pl.3.
Holborough Kent	grave 8	C2 31.3f	conical 8.5	knife, shield	Maidstone Museum	*Arch.Cantiana*, LXX, 1956, 121, fig.17,2.
Hollingbourne Kent	grave	C3 f)39.6f	-	-	Maidstone Museum	-
Hollingbourne Kent	grave	H2 f24.6f	-	-	Maidstone Museum	-
Hollingbourne Kent	grave	D1 f14.1f	-	-	Maidstone Museum	-
Hollingbourne Kent	grave	H1 f10.1f	-	-	Maidstone Museum	-
Holywell Row Suffolk	grave 38	H3 34.5(f	conical 8.1	knife, shield	Cambridge Museum Z.7122a	*Cambridge Ant.Soc.Quarto Pubs.*, III, 1931, 28.
Horton Kirby I Kent	grave	H1 16.1f	conical 9.2	knife	Maidstone Museum	-
Horton Kirby I Kent	grave	J f)21.0	-	-	Maidstone Museum 40 1933	-
Housesteads Northumberland	Roman Fort	A1 9.9f	-	-	Newcastle Museum 1956 151.66A	*Spearheads*, 146, fig.4b.
Howletts Kent	grave 3	D3 55.6	-	sword, shield	British Museum 1918 7-8 14	*PSA.*, 2nd S. XXX, 1917-8, 105.
Howletts Kent	grave	H3 56.0	-	-	British Museum 1918 7-8 15	*PSA.*, 2nd S. XXX, 1917-8, 105.

Provenance	Nature of find.	Type Length	Butt-ferrule	Associated weapons.	Museum Accession no.	Publication
Howletts Kent	grave	G2 35.5	-	-	British Museum 1918 7-8 16	*PSA.*, 2nd S. XXX, 1917-8, 105.
Howletts Kent	grave 32	F3 f)32.4	conical 13.4	-	British Museum 1936 5-11 118,119	*Spearheads*, 187.
Howletts Kent	grave 36	E3 46.9	conical 10.5	sword	British Museum 1936 5-11 133,153	-
		E3 27.0f	conical 6.9		British Museum 1936 5-11 134,154	-
Howletts Kent	grave	E3 46.7	-	-	British Museum 1936 5-11 149	-
Howletts Kent	grave	E4 39.8	-	-	British Museum 1936 5-11 150	-
Howletts Kent	grave	H2 27.7(f	-	-	British Museum 1936 5-11	-
Howletts Kent	grave	E3 f34.5f	-	-	British Museum 1936 5-11	-
Howletts Kent	grave	E3 f)39.2	-	-	British Museum 1936 5-11	-
Howletts Kent	grave	G2 f)38.0(f	-	-	British Museum 1936 5-11	-
Howletts Kent	grave	G2 f30.0f	-	-	British Museum 1936 5-11	-
Howletts Kent	grave	E2 f)20.5f	-	-	British Museum 1936 5-11	-
Howletts Kent	grave	E3 f42.9(f	-	-	British Museum 1936 5-11	-
Howletts Kent	grave	C3 36.7	-	-	Quex Park Museum 145 1914	-
Howletts Kent	grave	G2 f28.2f	-	-	Quex Park Museum 146 1914	-
Hunstanton Park Norfolk	grave	H2 25.4	-	-	Norwich Museum 1.2.950	-
Hunstanton Park Norfolk	grave	E4 f24.1	-	knife	Norwich Museum 1.2.950	-
Illington Norfolk	grave H1	E3 f)38.6	-	-	Norwich Museum 220.950	*Norfolk Archaeology*, XXXI, 1957, 406.
Ipswich Suffolk	grave	G2 f28.7f	-	-	Ipswich Museum 1907 29	-
Ipswich Suffolk	grave	E3 31.6f	-	-	Ipswich Museum 1907 29	-
Ipswich Suffolk	grave	G1 f)19.9f	-	-	Ipswich Museum 1907 29	-
Ipswich Suffolk	grave	G1 21.0f	-	-	Ipswich Museum 1907 29	-
Ipswich Suffolk	grave	G1 f)20.0f	-	-	Ipswich Museum 1907 29	-
Ipswich Suffolk	grave	G1 19.1(f	-	-	Ipswich Museum 1907 29	-
Ipswich Suffolk	grave	E3 f29.5(f	-	-	Ipswich Museum 1907 29	-
Ipswich Suffolk	grave	E4 f)25.4f	-	-	Ipswich Museum 1907 29	-
Ipswich Suffolk	grave	E3 30.0	-	-	Ipswich Museum 1907 29	-
Ipswich Suffolk	grave	E2 f)19.5f	-	-	Ipswich Museum 1907 29	-
Ipswich Suffolk	grave	G2 f26.1f	-	-	Ipswich Museum 1907 29	-
Ipswich Suffolk	grave	G2 30.4	-	-	Ipswich Museum 1907 29	-
Ipswich Suffolk	grave	H3 29.7f	-	-	Ipswich Museum 1907 29	-
Ipswich Suffolk	grave	E4 f34.8	-	-	Ipswich Museum 1907 29	-
Ipswich Suffolk	grave	C3 f26.7(f	-	-	Ipswich Museum 1907 29	-

Provenance	Nature of find.	Type Length	Butt-ferrule	Associated weapons.	Museum Accession no.	Publication
Ipswich Suffolk	grave	C4 f32.6f	-	-	Ipswich Museum 1907 29	-
Ipswich Suffolk	grave	E2 22.8	-	-	Ipswich Museum 1907 29	-
Ipswich Suffolk	grave	F2 f22.2	-	-	Ipswich Museum 1907 29	-
Ipswich Suffolk	grave	E3 f18.5	-	-	Ipswich Museum 1907 29	-
Ipswich Suffolk	grave	C2 f)22.0(f	-	-	Ipswich Museum 1907 29	-
Ipswich Suffolk	grave	F2 f23.8	-	-	Ipswich Museum 1907 29	-
Ipswich Suffolk	grave	C2 f32.7	-	-	Ipswich Museum 1907 29	-
Ipswich Suffolk	grave	E3 f)43.0	-	-	Ipswich Museum 1907 29	-
Ipswich Suffolk	grave	C2 f)49.1	-	-	Ipswich Museum 1907 29	-
Ipswich Suffolk	grave	E4 f)38.6	-	-	Ipswich Museum 1907 29	-
Ipswich Suffolk	grave	E3 38.8	-	-	Ipswich Museum 1907 29	-
Ipswich Suffolk	grave	E3 f)40.8	-	-	Ipswich Museum 1907 29	-
Ipswich Suffolk	grave	E3 f)29.2f	-	-	Ipswich Museum 1907 29	-
Ipswich Suffolk	grave	E3 f11.8f	-	-	Ipswich Museum 1907 29	-
Ipswich Suffolk	grave	E2 f11.7f	-	-	Ipswich Museum 1907 29	-
Ipswich Suffolk	grave	F2 f27.7	-	-	Ipswich Museum 1907 29	-
Ipswich Suffolk	grave	E3 f)24.3f	-	-	Ipswich Museum 1907 29	-
Ipswich Suffolk	grave	E4 f)47.6	-	-	Ipswich Museum 1907 29	-
Ipswich Suffolk	grave	F2 38.3	-	-	Ipswich Museum 1907 29	-
Ipswich Suffolk	grave	E1 f15.3f	-	-	Ipswich Museum 1907 29	-
Ipswich Suffolk	grvve	E3 45.0	-	-	Ipswich Museum 1907 29	-
Ipswich Suffolk	grave	E3 45.0	-	-	Ipswich Museum 1907 29	-
Ipswich Suffolk	grave	E3 54.3	-	-	Ipswich Museum 1907 29	-
Ipswich Suffolk	grave	E3 f)47.5f	-	-	Ipswich Museum 1907 29	-
Ipswich Suffolk	grave	G1 f14.1f	-	-	Ipswich Museum 1907 29	-
Ixworth Suffolk	-	E3 f26.1f	-	-	Ipswich Museum 1943 24-1	-
Ixworth Suffolk	-	B1 15.1f	-	-	Ipswich Museum 1943 24-2	-
Ixworth Thorpe Suffolk	grave	I2 26.8	-	sword, shield	Ipswich Museum 1947 86	*Spearheads*, 207, fig. 84e.
Kempston Beds.	grave	H1 17.2f	-	-	Bedford Museum 3782	-
Kempston Beds.	grave	H1 19.8	-	-	Bedford Museum 3783	-
Kempston Beds.	grave	C3 f)55.0f	-	-	Bedford Museum 3784	-
Kempston Beds.	grave	H1 19.0	-	-	Bedford Museum 3785	-
Kempston Beds.	grave	C2 f)28.3	-	-	Bedford Museum 3786	-

Provenance	Nature of find.	Type Length	Butt-ferrule	Associated weapons.	Museum Accession no.	Publication
Kempston Beds.	grave	C1 15.5	-	-	Bedford Museum BTC	-
Kempston Beds.	grave	H3 21.8f	-	-	British Museum 91 4-14 7	-
Kempston Beds.	grave	E3 39.9f	-	-	British Museum 91 6-24 81	-
Kempston Beds.	grave	E3 42.7	-	-	British Museum 91 6-24 82	*Spearheads*, fig. 27c.
Kempston Beds.	grave	H3 35.6	-	-	British Museum 91 6-24 83	-
Kempston Beds.	grave	H3 f)33.0	-	-	British Museum 91 6-24 84	-
Kempston Beds.	grave	H3 34.5	-	-	British Museum 91 6-24 85	-
Kempston Beds.	grave	I2 28.9	-	-	British Museum 91 6-24 86	*Spearheads*, fig. 47e.
Kempston Beds.	grave	E2 f)25.9	-	-	British Museum 91 6-24 87	-
Kempston Beds.	grave	H2 f)22.5	-	-	British Museum 91 6-24 88	-
Kempston Beds.	grave	C5 29.7	-	-	British Museum 91 6-24 89	*Spearheads*, fig. 16b.
Kempston Beds.	grave	H2 25.2	-	-	British Museum 91 6-24 90	-
Kempston Beds.	grave	H2 f19.1	-	-	British Museum 91 6-24 91	-
Kempston Beds.	grave	H2 24.6	-	-	British Museum 91 6-24 92	-
Kempston Beds.	grave	L f)35.2	-	-	British Museum 91 6-24 93	-
Kempston Beds.	grave	F1 21.5	-	-	British Museum 91 6-24 94	-
Kempston Beds.	grave	H1 15.6	-	-	British Museum 91 6-24 95	-
Kempston Beds.	grave	H1 15.7	-	-	British Museum 91 6-24 96	-
Kempston Beds.	grave	E1 f)12.8	-	-	British Museum 91 6-24 97	-
Kempston Beds.	grave	H1 f)13.2	-	-	British Museum 91 6-24 98	-
Kempston Beds.	grave	E1 f)16.2	-	-	British Museum 91 6-24 99	-
Kempston Beds.	grave	L 18.4	-	-	British Museum 91 6-24 100	-
Kempston Beds.	grave	H1 f)20.9	-	-	British Museum 91 6-24 101	-
Kempston Beds.	grave	J 26.3	-	-	British Museum 91 6-24 102	-
Kent	-	C2 f23.1(f	-	-	Maidstone Museum	-
Kent	-	C1 16.7	-	-	Maidstone Museum	-
Kent	-	C4 f29.4f	-	-	Maidstone Museum	-
Kew Surrey	River Thames	E1 13.8	-	-	London Museum A.13549	-
Kew Surrey	River Thames	H1 13.8	-	-	London Museum A.13550	-
Kidlington Oxon.	River Cherwell	C2 26.1	-	-	Ashmolean Museum 1938 879	-
Kilham Yorks.	grave	H3 31.8	-	-	York Museum 396.47	*Spearheads*, fig. 41c.
Kilham Yorks.	grave	C1 f16.0	-	-	York Museum 397.47	-
Kilham Yorks.	grave	D1 f)18.6(f	-	-	York Museum 398.47	-

Provenance	Nature of find.	Type Length	Butt-ferrule	Associated weapons.	Museum Accession no.	Publication
Kingston Kent	grave 2	E3 53.0	-	shield	-	*Faussett Papers.*
Kingston Kent	grave 3	D2 31.7	*	knife, ?arrow	-	*Faussett Papers.*
Kingston Kent	grave 4	D2 c30.0	-	-	-	*Faussett Papers.*
Kingston Kent	grave 16	C2 33.4	-	sword, shield	-	*Inventorium Sepulchrale,* 45, pl. xiv.
Kingston Kent	grave 94	E1 7.6	-	knife	-	*Faussett Papers.*
Kingston Kent	grave 129	D2 c56.0	cylindrical 0.5	shield	-	*Faussett Papers.*
Kingston Kent	grave 140	D2 c53.0	-	knife, shield	-	*Faussett Papers.*
Kingston Kent	grave 163	E3 c53.0	cylindrical 2.5	knife, shield another spear	-	*Faussett Papers.*
Kingston Kent	grave 173	B1 27.3(f	-	knife	Liverpool Museum 6263	*Inventorium Sepulchrale,* 45, pl. xiv,8.
Kingston Kent	grave	D2 31.0	-	-	Liverpool Museum 6305	-
Kingston Kent	grave	E2 f)27.6	-	-	Liverpool Museum	-
Kingston Surrey	River Thames	D3 27.8	-	-	London Museum A.26666	-
Kingston Surrey	River Thames	L 28.4	-	-	London Museum A.27422	-
Kingston Surrey	-	D2 33.1	-	-	Kingston Museum 30.4	-
Kingston Surrey	-	A1 35.8	-	-	Kingston Museum 378	-
Kingston Surrey	-	B2 43.3	-	-	Kingston Museum 408	-
Kingston Surrey	River Thames	F2 21.0f	-	-	Kingston Museum 824	-
Kingston Surrey	River Thames	C1 11.4f	-	-	Kingston Museum 825	-
Kingston Surrey	River Thames	E2 21.0	-	-	Reading Museum 279.47	-
Kinsey Oxon.	grave	H1 18.8	-	-	Aylesbury Museum 4.60	*Records of Bucks.*, II, 1863, 166, fig.2.
Kinsey Oxon.	grave	H2 26.4	-	-	Taunton Museum A.888	*VCH. Oxon.*, I, 352.
Kirton-in-Lindsey II, Lincs.	grave	C5 24.4f	-	2 knives, seax, sword	Lincoln Museum 7.11.24	*Spearheads*, 169.
Laceby Lincs.	grave	E2 f)19.0f	conical 15.3	-	Lincoln Museum 19.20	*Antiqu.Journal*, XXXVI, 1956, 181.
Laceby Lincs.	grave	G1 f24.9	-	knife	Lincoln Museum 3.34	-
Laceby Lincs.	grave	E1 16.8	-	-	Lincoln Museum 99.54	*Spearheads*, fig. 23d.
Lambeth London	River Thames	D1 16.2	-	-	British Museum 56 7-1 1454	-
Lancing Sussex	grave	H2 f18.9(f	-	-	-	*Sussex Arch.Collections,* LXXXI, 1940, 171-2, fig.18,1.
Lancing Sussex	grave	H2 22.7	-	-	-	*Sussex Arch.Collections,* LXXXI, 1940, 172, fig.18,2.
Leighton Buzzard I, Beds.	grave 5	G2 44.0	-	2 knives	Luton Museum	*Arch.Journal*, CXX, 1963, 167, fig. 6a.
Leighton Buzzard I, Beds.	grave 17	F2 29.1	-	2 knives	Luton Museum	*Arch.Journal*, CXX, 1963, 171, fig. 6b.
Letchworth Herts.	grave 1	D1 24.8	-	-	Letchworth Museum	-
Lewes Sussex	grave	E2 f)17.7	-	-	British Museum 53 4-12 83	-
		H1 19.4(f	-	-	British Museum 53 4-12 84	-

Provenance	Nature of find.	Type Length	Butt-ferrule	Associated weapons.	Museum Accession no.	Publication
Lewes Sussex	grave	A1 17.8	-	-	British Museum 53 4-12 139	-
Lewes Sussex	-	K2 22.9	-	-	Lewes Museum 235	-
Lincoln Lincs.	-	E2 21.5	-	-	British Museum 66 12-3 198	-
Linton Heath B Cambs.	grave 2	H2 f)24.6	-	-	Cambridge Museum 48.1513	Arch.Journal, XI, 1854, 96.
Linton Heath B Cambs.	grave 7	H3 32.5	-	knife, shield	Cambridge Museum 48.1517a	Arch.Journal, XI, 1854, 96.
Linton Heath B Cambs.	grave 13	H3 35.4	-	-	Cambridge Museum 48.1527	Arch.Journal, XI, 1854, 98.
Linton Heath B Cambs.	grave 23	H1 14.7	-	knife	Cambridge Museum 48.1544	Arch.Journal, XI, 1854, 101.
Linton Heath B Cambs.	grave 46	E3 56.5	-	shield	Cambridge Museum 48.1578	Arch.Journal, XI, 1854, 105, fig. i.
Linton Heath B Cambs.	grave 48	E3 29.1f	-	-	Cambridge Museum 48.1581	Arch.Journal, XI, 1854, 106.
Linton Heath B Cambs.	grave 66	E1 20.9	-	-	Cambridge Museum 48.1591	Arch.Journal, XI, 1854, 108, fig. ii.
Linton Heath B Cambs.	grave 80	H1 13.1(f	-	-	Cambridge Museum 48.1605	Arch.Journal, XI, 1854, 110.
Linton Heath B Cambs.	grave 81	E2 23.8	-	knife, shield	Cambridge Museum 48.1606	Arch.Journal, XI, 1854, 110, fig. iv.
Linton Heath B Cambs.	grave 89	C1 15.9	-	-	Cambridge Museum 48.1612	Arch.Journal, XI, 1854, 111.
Linton Heath B Cambs.	grave 95	H1 19.1	-	-	Cambridge Museum 48.1618	Arch.Journal, XI, 1854, 112.
Linton Heath B Cambs.	grave 102	E1 13.3	-	-	Cambridge Museum 48.1624	Arch.Journal, XI, 1854, 113.
Linton Heath B Cambs.	grave	L 27.6	-	-	Cambridge Museum 48.1535	-
Linton Heath Cambs.	grave	H1 f)16.4	-	-	Cambridge Museum 48.1642	-
Linton Heath B Cambs.	grave	H1 22.0	-	-	Cambridge Museum 48.1642	-
Linton Heath B Cambs.	grave	H1 14.0f	-	-	Cambridge Museum 48.1642	-
Linton Heath B Cambs.	grave	H1 18.3	-	-	Cambridge Museum 48.1642	-
Linton Heath B Cambs.	grave	E3 f24.1	-	-	Cambridge Museum 48.1642	-
Linton Heath B Cambs.	grave	E2 f16.2	-	-	Cambridge Museum 48.1642	-
Linton Heath B Cambs.	grave	H3 30.5	-	-	Cambridge Museum 48.1642	-
Linton Heath B Cambs.	grave	H1 20.3	-	-	Cambridge Museum 48.1644	-
Linton Heath B Cambs.	grave	C2 21.0	-	-	Cambridge Museum 48.1644	-
Linton Heath B Cambs.	grave	C2 30.7	-	-	Cambridge Museum 48.1644	-
Little Hinton Wilts.	surface find	C1 16.5	-	-	Ashmolean Museum 1955 364e	-
Little Wilbraham Cambs.	grave A	H2 22.1	-	knife, shield	-	Arch.Journal, VII, 1851, 173, fig.
Little Wilbraham Cambs.	grave 28	E3 46.0	-	knife	-	Saxon Obsequies, 15.
Little Wilbraham Cambs.	grave 77	E3 45.5	-	knife, shield	-	Saxon Obsequies, 18, pl. 35.
Little Wilbraham Cambs.	grave	C1 17.4	-	-	Cambridge Museum 48.1636	-
Little Wilbraham Cambs.	grave	E1 16.6	-	-	Cambridge Museum 48.1636	-
Little Wilbraham Cambs.	grave	D1 f19.3	-	-	Cambridge Museum 48.1636	-

Provenance	Nature of find.	Type Length	Butt-ferrule	Associated weapons.	Museum Accession no.	Publication
Little Wilbraham Cambs.	grave	E2 f)22.7f	-	-	Cambridge Museum 48.1636	-
Little Wilbraham Cambs.	grave	L 31.7	-	-	Cambridge Museum 48.1636	-
Little Wilbraham Cambs.	grave	F2 f)28.2	-	-	Cambridge Museum 48.1636	-
Little Wilbraham Cambs.	grave	H3 32.9	-	-	Cambridge Museum 48.1636	-
Little Wilbraham Cambs.	grave	E3 f)33.5f	-	-	Cambridge Museum 48.1636	-
Little Wilbraham Cambs.	grave	D3 22.5(f	-	-	Cambridge Museum 48.1639	*Spearheads*, fig. 21b.
Little Wilbraham Cambs.	grave	D1 16.5	-	-	Cambridge Museum 48.1640	*Spearheads*, fig. 18c.
Little Wilbraham Cambs.	grave	D1 19.1	-	-	Cambridge Museum 48.1640	-
Little Wilbraham Cambs.	grave	C1 17.7	-	-	Cambridge Museum 48.1640	-
Little Wilbraham Cambs.	grave	E1 f15.4	-	-	Cambridge Museum 48.1640	-
Little Wilbraham Cambs.	grave	E1 f12.7	-	-	Cambridge Museum 48.1640	-
Little Wilbraham Cambs.	grave	F1 f14.9	-	-	Cambridge Museum 48.1640	-
Little Wilbraham Cambs.	grave	F1 f15.1	-	-	Cambridge Museum 48.1640	-
Little Wilbraham Cambs.	grave	E1 12.7	-	-	Cambridge Museum 48.1640	-
Little Wilbraham Cambs.	grave	D1 f)28.2	-	-	Cambridge Museum 48.1641	-
Little Wilbraham Cambs.	grave	H3 f)28.3	-	-	Cambridge Museum 48.1641	-
Little Wilbraham Cambs.	grave	C3 f23.8f	-	-	Cambridge Museum 48.1641	-
Little Wilbraham Cambs.	grave	H3 f)35.5	-	-	Cambridge Museum 48.1641	-
Loddington Northants.	grave	C2 f18.7f	-	shield	Northampton Museum D.293	*Antiqu.Journal*, XLIII, 1963, 46, fig. 25c.
Loddington Northants.	grave	C3 33.7	-	shield	Northampton Museum D.294	*Antiqu.Journal*, XLIII, 1963, 46, fig. 25d.
Londesborough Yorks.	grave 8	C1 10.1(f	-	knife, seax	Hull Museum	*Yorks.Arch.Journal*, XLI, 1964, 276, fig.2,5.
London	River Thames	B2 f43.3f	-	-	British Museum 56 7-1 1431	-
London	-	E4 f23.4(f	-	-	British Museum 56 7-1 1453	-
London	-	E2 21.2f	-	-	British Museum 56 7-1 -455	-
London	River Thames	I2 24.4	-	-	Guildhall Museum, London, 4055	-
London	-	E3 42.0	-	-	Guildhall Museum, London, 22022	-
London	-	K1 19.0f	-	-	London Museum 29.94.13	*London & the Saxons*, 169, fig. 39,7.
London	River Thames	H2 21.6	-	-	London Museum A.14912	*London & the Saxons*, 163, pl. ix,8.
London	River Thames	E1 16.7	-	-	London Museum B.328	*London & the Saxons*, 163, pl. ix,9.
London	River Thames	C2 24.7f	-	-	London Museum C.742	-
Longbridge Park Warwicks.	grave	C2 31.9	-	-	British Museum 80 5-21 3	*Spearheads*, fig. 11c.
Longbridge Park Warwicks.	grave	H3 32.4	-	-	British Museum 80 5-21 4	-
Longbridge Park Warwicks.	grave	E3 f)31.2	-	-	British Museum 80 5-21 5	-

Provenance	Nature of find.	Type Length	Butt-ferrule	Associated weapons.	Museum Accession no.	Publication
Longbridge Park Warwicks.	grave	E2 24.1	-	-	British Museum 80 5-21 6	-
Longbridge Park Warwicks.	grave	H1 f)12.1f	-	-	British Museum 80 5-21 7	-
Longbridge Park Warwicks.	grave	G2 f)23.4f	-	-	British Museum 80 5-21 8	-
Longbridge Park Warwicks.	grave	E1 f12.2f	-	-	British Museum 80 5-21 9	-
Long Wittenham I Berks.	grave A	K1 f)28.2	-	knife, sword shield	Ashmolean Museum PR.454	Arch.Journal, V, 1848, 292, fig.
Long Wittenham I Berks.	grave 8	E1 14.9	-	knife	British Museum 75 3-10 74	Archaeologia, XXXVIII, 1860, 338.
Long Wittenham I Berks.	grave 9	H1 f)20.7	-	2 knives, shield	British Museum 75 3-10 75	Archaeologia, XXXVIII, 1860, 338.
Long Wittenham I Berks.	grave 21	L 26.8	*	knife	British Museum 62 6-13 95	Archaeologia, XXXVIII, 1860, 338.
Long Wittenham I Berks.	grave 24	C1 f)15.0	-	knife	British Museum 75 3-10 101	Archaeologia, XXXVIII, 1860, 339.
Long Wittenham I Berks.	grave 25	E1 f23.1	-	knife, shield	British Museum 75 3-10 104	Archaeologia, XXXVIII, 1860, 339.
Long Wittenham I Berks.	grave 26	H2 27.8	cast bronze 9.4	shield	British Museum 75 3-10 109,110	Archaeologia, XXXVIII, 1860, 339, fig.
Long Wittenham I Berks.	grave 36	H1 20.4	-	knife, shield	British Museum 75 3-10 139	Archaeologia, XXXVIII, 1860, 340.
		H2 28.3	-		British Museum 75 3-10 326	Archaeologia, XXXVIII, 1860, 340.
Long Wittenham I Berks.	grave 38	C3 34.5	-	-	British Museum 75 3-10 140	Archaeologia, XXXVIII, 1860, 340.
Long Wittenham I Berks.	grave 42	K1 f)22.3	-	knife, shield	British Museum 75 3-10 141	Archaeologia, XXXVIII, 1860, 340.
Long Wittenham I Berks.	grave 44	E1 17.3	-	knife	British Museum 75 3-10 144	Archaeologia, XXXVIII, 1860, 340.
Long Wittenham I Berks.	grave 48	H2 19.2	-	shield	British Museum 75 3-10 158	Archaeologia, XXXVIII, 1860, 341.
Long Wittenham I Berks.	grave 56	H1 15.6	-	knife, shield	British Museum 75 3-10 169	Archaeologia, XXXVIII, 1860, 342.
Long Wittenham I Berks.	grave 60	H1 16.7	-	knife	British Museum 75 3-10 174	Archaeologia, XXXVIII, 1860, 342.
Long Wittenham I Berks.	grave 61	H2 28.3	-	knife	British Museum 75 3-10 175	Archaeologia, XXXVIII, 1860, 342.
Long Wittenham I Berks.	grave 64	E1 f)18.2	-	-	British Museum 75 3-10 178	Archaeologia, XXXVIII, 1860, 342.
Long Wittenham I Berks.	grave 66	E1 f)19.5(f	-	knife	British Museum 75 3-10 182	Archaeologia, XXXVIII, 1860, 343.
Long Wittenham I Berks.	grave 67	H3 41.1	-	sword, shield	British Museum 75 3-10 186	Archaeologia, XXXVIII, 1860, 343.
Long Wittenham I Berks.	grave 69	C1 15.1	-	-	British Museum 75 3-10 202	Archaeologia, XXXVIII, 1860, 343.
Long Wittenham I Berks.	grave 74	F2 f)12.0	-	knife	British Museum 75 3-10 209	Archaeologia, XXXVIII, 1860, 343.
Long Wittenham I Berks.	grave 76	E1 f)15.9	-	knife	British Museum 75 3-10 210	Archaeologia, XXXVIII, 1860, 343.
Long Wittenham I Berks.	grave 81	H1 20.0	-	knife, shield	British Museum 75 3-10 220	Archaeologia, XXXVIII, 1860, 344.
Long Wittenham I Berks.	grave 82	H2 28.0	-	shield	British Museum 75 3-10 223	Archaeologia, XXXVIII, 1860, 344.
Long Wittenham I Berks.	grave 83	C2 f)18.7	-	shield	British Museum 75 3-10 226	Archaeologia, XXXVIII, 1860, 344.
Long Wittenham I Berks.	grave 91	H2 29.0	-	shield	British Museum 75 3-10 233	Archaeologia, XXXVIII, 1860, 345.
Long Wittenham I Berks.	grave 92	H2 24.2	-	shield	British Museum 75 3-10 236	Archaeologia, XXXVIII, 1860, 345.
Long Wittenham I Berks.	grave 93	E1 14.8	-	knife	British Museum 75 3-10 238	Archaeologia, XXXVIII, 1860, 345.

Provenance	Nature of find.	Type Length	Butt-ferrule	Associated weapons.	Museum Accession no.	Publication
Long Wittenham I Berks.	grave 106	E1 21.2	-	shield	British Museum 75 3-10 264	*Archaeologia*, XXXVIII, 1860, 346.
		F1 17.8	-		British Museum 75 3-10 265	*Archaeologia*, XXXVIII, 1860, 346.
Long Wittenham I Berks.	grave 107	C2 24.5	-	shield	British Museum 75 3-10 266	*Archaeologia*, XXXVIII, 1860, 346.
Long Wittenham I Berks.	grave 112	E1 18.7	-	-	British Museum 75 3-10 302	*Archaeologia*, XXXVIII, 1860, 347.
Long Wittenham I Berks.	grave 114	C2 19.0(f	-	-	British Museum 75 3-10 306	*Archaeologia*, XXXVIII, 1860, 347.
Long Wittenham I Berks.	grave 118	H2 27.6	-	-	British Museum 75 3-10 310	*Archaeologia*, XXXVIII, 1860, 347.
Long Wittenham I Berks.	grave 126	C2 23.0	-	shield	British Museum 75 3-10 322	*Archaeologia*, XXXVIII, 1860, 348.
Long Wittenham I Berks.	grave 128	H1 18.0	-	knife	British Museum 62 6-13 1	*Archaeologia*, XXXIX, 1861, 138.
Long Wittenham I Berks.	grave 131	H2 21.1	-	knife	British Museum 62 6-13 8	*Archaeologia*, XXXIX, 1861, 139.
Long Wittenham I Berks.	grave 138	H1 20.3	-	knife, shield	British Museum 62 6-13 20	*Archaeologia*, XXXIX, 1861, 139.
Long Wittenham I Berks.	grave 146	H2 26.0	-	knife, shield	British Museum 62 6-13 30	*Archaeologia*, XXXIX, 1861, 140.
Long Wittenham I Berks.	grave 154	E1 14.0	-	knife	British Museum 62 6-13 53	*Archaeologia*, XXXIX, 1861, 140.
Long Wittenham I Berks.	grave 155	E1 13.0	-	knife	British Museum 62 6-13 54	*Archaeologia*, XXXIX, 1861, 140.
Long Wittenham I Berks.	grave 161	E3 32.5	-	knife, shield	British Museum 62 6-13 59	*Archaeologia*, XXXIX, 1861, 140.
Long Wittenham I Berks.	grave 168	H1 19.5	-	knife, shield	British Museum 62 6-13 78	*Archaeologia*, XXXIX, 1861, 141.
Long Wittenham I Berks.	grave 174	E3 37.6	-	-	British Museum 62 6-13 86	*Archaeologia*, XXXIX, 1861, 141.
		F1 f)19.9	-	-	British Museum 62 6-13 87	*Archaeologia*, XXXIX, 1861, 141.
Long Wittenham I Berks.	grave 175	E2 22.7f	-	-	British Museum 62 6-13 88	*Archaeologia*, XXXIX, 1861, 141.
Long Wittenham I Berks.	grave 176	C2 f24.7	-	-	British Museum 62 6-13 90	*Archaeologia*, XXXIX, 1861, 141.
Long Wittenham I Berks.	grave 179	H2 21.4	-	knife, shield	British Museum 62 6-13 94	*Archaeologia*, XXXIX, 1861, 141.
Long Wittenham I Berks.	grave 180a	D3 13.3	-	shield	British Museum 62 6-13 97	*Archaeologia*, XXXIX, 1861, 141.
Long Wittenham I Berks.	grave 180b	E3 33.7	-	-	British Museum 62 6-13 98	*Archaeologia*, XXXIX, 1861, 141.
Long Wittenham I Berks.	grave	H2 26.0	-	-	British Museum	-
Long Wittenham I Berks.	grave	H1 f)18.5	-	-	British Museum	-
Long Wittenham I Berks.	grave	H2 25.9	-	-	British Museum	*Spearheads*, fig. 39d.
Long Wittenham I Berks.	grave	E1 f)13.2	-	-	British Museum	-
Long Wittenham I Berks.	grave	H1 19.8	-	-	British Museum	-
Long Wittenham I Berks.	grave	C2 23.0	-	-	British Museum	-
Long Wittenham I Berks.	grave	E1 f11.3f	-	-	British Museum	-
Long Wittenham I Berks.	grave	H3 f)30.1(f	-	-	British Museum	-
Loveden Hill Lincs.	cremation 1	C2 22.0	-	sword	Lincoln Museum	*Spearheads*, 159.
Loveden Hill Lincs.	grave 3	E3 40.6	-	-	Lincoln Museum 22.57	-
Lowbury Berks.	grave	C2 19.8f	-	knife, sword, shield	Reading University History Department	Atkinson, 16, 21, pl.iv.

Provenance	Nature of find.	Type Length	Butt-ferrule	Associated weapons.	Museum Accession no.	Publication
Lowesby Hall Leics.	grave	C2 29.5	-	-	Leicester Museum 49 1852	-
Lowesby Hall Leics.	grave	E4 f)58.0f	-	sword	Leicester Museum 80 1854	PSA., II, 1853, 255.
		F3 f)18.0(f	-		Leicester Museum 80 1854	PSA., II, 1853, 255.
Luton I Beds.	grave	I2 28.8	-	knife	Luton Museum 113.52	Antiqu.Journal, VIII, 1928, 178.
Luton I Beds.	grave 6	C1 f)13.2	-	knife	Luton Museum BL.47.33	Antiqu.Journal, VIII, 1928, 186, pl.34.2,6.
Luton I Beds.	grave 11	F1 14.6	-	shield	-	Antiqu.Journal, VIII, 1928, 187, pl.34.1,5.
		H1 12.1f	-		-	Antiqu.Journal, VIII, 1928, 187, pl.34.1,7.
Luton I Beds.	grave 14	H1 20.5	-	-	Luton Museum BL.53.33	Antiqu.Journal, VIII, 1928, pl. 34.2,3.
Luton I Beds.	cremation 20	D1 23.8	-	-	Luton Museum	Antiqu.Journal, VIII, 1928, 188, pl.34.1,3.
Luton I Beds.	grave 21	H3 36.4	-	knife, shield	Luton Museum	Antiqu.Journal, VIII, 1928, 188, pl.34.2,8.
Luton I Beds.	grave 24	H1 f)12.1	-	-	Luton Museum BL.31.41	Antiqu.Journal, VIII, 1928, 190, pl.34.2,5.
Luton I Beds.	grave 32	D1 15.8	-	knife	Luton Museum BL.89.33	Antiqu.Journal, VIII, 1928, 191, pl.35,16.
Luton I Beds.	grave	H2 27.0	-	-	-	Antiqu.Journal, VIII, 1928, pl.34.1,1.
Luton I Beds.	grave	H2 24.4	-	-	-	Antiqu.Journal, VIII, 1928, pl.34.1,2.
Luton I Beds.	grave	H1 f)16.9	-	-	Luton Museum BL.103.33	Antiqu.Journal, VIII, 1928, pl.34.1,4.
Luton I Beds.	grave	C1 13.4	-	-	-	Antiqu.Journal, VIII, 1928, pl.34.1,6.
Luton I Beds.	grave	H2 26.0	-	-	-	Antiqu.Journal, VIII, 1928, pl.34.2,1.
Luton I Beds.	grave	H2 23.3	-	-	Luton Museum BL.101.33	Antiqu.Journal, VIII, 1928, pl.34.2,2.
Luton I Beds.	grave	H1 19.8	-	-	Luton Museum BL.102.33	Antiqu.Journal, VIII, 1928, pl.34.2,4.
Luton I Beds.	grave	E1 12.0	-	-	-	Antiqu.Journal, VIII, 1928, pl.34.2,7.
Luton I Beds.	grave	D1 23.8	-	-	-	Antiqu.Journal, VI, 1926, 184, fig.1.
Luton I Beds.	grave	H1 20.4	-	-	-	Antiqu.Journal, VI, 1926, 184, fig.1.
Luton I Beds.	grave	H2 26.3	-	-	Luton Museum BL.32.41	-
Luton I Beds.	grave	H2 26.6	-	-	Luton Museum BL.33.41	-
Luton I Beds.	grave	H2 f)23.9	-	-	Luton Museum BL.5.45	-
Luton I Beds.	grave	F1 f)15.1	-	-	Luton Museum	Spearheads, fig. 31d.
Luton I Beds.	grave	H1 15.0	-	-	Luton Museum BL.30.41-7	-
Luton I Beds.	grave	H2 24.5	-	-	Luton Museum BL.34.31	-
Luton I Beds.	grave	E1 f12.3	-	-	Luton Museum BL.104.33	Spearheads, fig. 23c.
Luton I Beds.	grave	H2 f)26.5	-	-	Luton Museum BL.137.32	-
Luton I Beds.	grave	C3 26.2	-	-	Luton Museum BL.2.10650	-
Luton I Beds.	grave	K2 f)24.9	-	-	Luton Museum	Spearheads, fig. 52d.

Provenance	Nature of find.	Type Length	Butt-ferrule	Associated weapons.	Museum Accession no.	Publication
Luton I Beds.	grave	H1 19.5	-	knife	Bedford Museum 3787	-
		H1 11.8f	-		Bedford Museum 3788	-
Lyminge II Kent	grave 1	H2 18.0f	*	knife, axe, shield	Maidstone Museum	Arch.Cantiana, LXIX, 1955, 7, fig. 3,2.
Lyminge II Kent	grave 4	H3 f)32.2	*	knife, shield	Maidstone Museum	Arch.Cantiana, LXIX, 1955, 9, fig. 3,5.
Lyminge II Kent	grave 5	H3 40.9	-	-	Maidstone Museum	Arch.Cantiana, LXIX, 1955, 9, fig. 3,6.
Lyminge II Kent	grave 6	D1 14.0f	-	knife	-	Arch.Cantiana, LXIX, 1955, 10, fig. 4,3.
Lyminge II Kent	grave 31	D3 23.5	-	knife, shield	-	Arch.Cantiana, LXIX, 1955, 22, fig. 4,7.
Lyneham Oxon.	grave 1	C2 24.7	-	knife	Ashmolean Museum 1922 269	PSA., 2nd S. XV, 1895, 406.
Lyneham Oxon.	grave	L 21.0	-	-	Ashmolean Museum 1922 273	-
Lyneham Oxon.	grave	H1 f)21.0	-	-	Ashmolean Museum 1922 274	-
Malling Hill Sussex	grave	C4 48.4	-	-	British Museum 53 4-12 77	-
Malling Hill Sussex	grave	C2 28.0	-	-	British Museum 53 4-12 78	-
Malling Hill Sussex	grave	F2 28.0(f	-	-	British Museum 53 4-12 79	Spearheads, fig. 32b.
Malling Hill Sussex	grave	E3 28.2f	-	-	British Museum 53 4-12 80	-
Malling Hill Sussex	grave	H1 21.4	-	-	British Museum 53 4-12 81	-
Market Overton Rutland	grave	E2 f20.4f	-	-	Oakham School	-
Market Overton Rutland	grave	E3 f29.9	-	-	Oakham School	-
Market Overton Rutland	grave	C2 f)25.5	-	-	Oakham School	-
Market Overton Rutland	grave	E3 f)32.9(f	-	-	Oakham School	-
Market Overton Rutland	grave	E2 18.2f	-	-	Oakham School	-
Market Overton Rutland	grave	C2 f)21.0	-	-	Oakham School	-
Market Overton Rutland	grave	H3 f)31.9(f	-	-	Oakham School	-
Market Overton Rutland	grave	G2 f23.4f	-	-	Oakham School	-
Market Overton Rutland	grave	E3 f48.2	-	-	Oakham School	-
Market Overton Rutland	grave	E4 35.3f	-	-	Oakham School	-
Market Overton Rutland	grave	E2 f)21.4(f	-	-	Oakham School	-
Market Overton Rutland	grave	H3 f)32.5(f	-	-	Oakham School	-
Market Overton Rutland	grave	E2 f)26.9f	-	-	Oakham School	-
Market Overton Rutland	grave	C2 f)16.0f	-	-	Oakham School	-
Market Overton Rutland	grave	C1 f15.3	-	-	Oakham School	-
Marlborough Wilts.	grave	K1 16.0	-	-	Ashmolean Museum 1955 3659	-
Marlow Bucks.	River Thames	I2 26.1(f	-	-	Toronto Museum 910.153.6	-
Marston St Lawrence, Northants.	grave 13	H2 27.8	-	shield	-	Archaeologia, XLVIII, 1882, 329, pl. xxv.

Provenance	Nature of find.	Type Length	Butt-ferrule	Associated weapons.	Museum Accession no.	Publication
Marston St Lawrence, Northants.	grave 16	K2 29.5	-	knife, seax	-	Archaeologia, XLVIII, 1882, 329, pl.xxv.
Marston St Lawrence, Northants.	grave 29	C2 24.0	conical 6.3	shield	-	Archaeologia, XLVIII, 1882, 330, pl.xxv.
		C2 24.0	-		-	Archaeologia, XLVIII, 1882, 330, pl.xxv.
Marston St Lawrence, Northants.	grave 30	H3 41.0	-	knife, shield	-	Archaeologia, XLVIII, 1882, 330, pl.xxv.
Marston St Lawrence, Northants.	grave 37	C2 24.5	-	knife	-	Archaeologia, XLVIII, 1882, 330, pl.xxv.
		C1 12.0	-		-	Archaeologia, XLVIII, 1882, 330, pl.xxv.
Matlock Derbs.	-	C1 17.8	-	-	Derby Museum	-
Melbourn Cambs.	grave 12	C3 f45.9	-	knife, shield	Cambridge Museum 53.190	Proc.Cambridge Ant.Soc., XLIX, 1956, 35, fig. 3.
Melbourn Cambs.	grave 25	C2 34.0	-	knife	Cambridge Museum 53.200	Proc.Cambridge Ant.Soc., XLIX, 1956, 37, fig. 4.
Melton Mowbray Leics.	grave 1	A2 57.5	-	knife, shield	-	Trans.Leics.Arch.Soc., III, 1874, 116.
Melton Mowbray Leics.	grave	C2 22.9	-	-	Leicester Museum 64 1870	-
Melton Mowbray Leics.	grave	E3 53.4	-	-	Leicester Museum 64 1870	-
Melton Mowbray Leics.	grave	H1 19.6	-	-	Leicester Museum 64 1870	-
Melton Mowbray Leics.	grave	E4 35.5(f	-	-	Leicester Museum 67 1870	Spearheads, fig. 29d.
Meols Cheshire	foreshore	D3 31.6	-	-	Chester Museum	Trans.H.S.Lancs.& Chesh., CXII, 1960, 21, fig.6d.
Meols Cheshire	foreshore	K2 f)19.0	-	-	Chester Museum	-
Merrow Surrey	?grave	L 30.8	-	-	Guildford Museum G.3810	Spearheads, 137, fig.53d.
Middle Wallop Wilts. Hants.	grave	F2 25.1	-	knife	Salisbury Museum 71.57	Salisbury Museum Report, 1957, 14-5.
Milton Berks.	grave	C2 27.9	-	-	Ashmolean Museum 1836 52	-
Milton Berks.	grave	H2 25.3	-	-	Ashmolean Museum 1836 52	-
Milton Berks.	grave	E2 f21.1	-	-	Ashmolean Museum	-
Milton Berks.	grave	E2 32.8	-	-	British Museum 62 7-19 3	-
Milton Berks.	grave	C3 32.8f	-	-	British Museum 62 7-19 4	-
Milton II Kent	grave	E3 f23.1(f	-	-	British Museum 83 11-13 630	-
Milton II Kent	grave	E2 15.1f	-	-	British Museum 83 12-13 631	-
Milton II Kent	grave	F2 20.3f	-	-	British Museum 83 12-13 632	-
Milton II Kent	grave	H2 23.3f	-	-	British Museum 83 12-13 633	-
Milton II Kent	grave	C2 20.6	-	-	British Museum 83 12-13 634	-
Milton II Kent	grave	F2 26.3	-	-	British Museum 83 12-13 635	-
Minnis Bay Kent	-	C2 26.5	-	-	Quex Park Museum 189	-
Minster Lovell Oxon.	grave	H2 20.4	-	knife, shield	Ashmolean Museum 1886 1447	VCH.Oxon., I, 367.
Mitcham Surrey	grave 27	E1 c20.0	-	knife, sword, shield	-	Surrey Arch.Collections, LVI, 1959, 59, 122.

Provenance	Nature of find	Type Length	Butt-ferrule	Associated weapons.	Museum Accession no.	Publication
Mitcham Surrey	grave 50	E1 c20.0	-	knife	-	*Surrey Arch.Collections*, LVI, 1959, 63, 122.
		E1 c20.0	-		-	*Surrey Arch.Collections*, LVI, 1959, 63, 122.
Mitcham Surrey	grave 51	C1 c13.0	-	-	-	*Surrey Arch.Collections*, LVI, 1959, 63, 122.
Mitcham Surrey	grave 54	E3 c30.0	-	-	-	*Surrey Arch.Collections*, LVI, 1959, 63, 122.
Mitcham Surrey	grave 58	H1 c15.0	-	-	-	*Surrey Arch.Collections*, LVI, 1959, 63, 122.
Mitcham Surrey	grave 60	E1 c15.0	-	-	-	*Surrey Arch.Collections*, LVI, 1959, 64, 122.
Mitcham Surrey	grave 63	H2 28.7	-	knife	London Museum 56.106.11	*Surrey Arch.Collections*, LVI, 1959, 64, 122.
Mitcham Surrey	grave 65	E1 c15.0	-	knife, sword, shield	-	*Surrey Arch.Collections*, LVI, 1959, 64, 122.
Mitcham Surrey	grave 73	E3 c33.0	-	knife, sword, shield	-	*Surrey Arch.Collections*, LVI, 1959, 65, 122.
Mitcham Surrey	grave 90	E2 c28.0	-	-	-	*Surrey Arch.Collections*, LVI, 1959, 66, 122.
Mitcham Surrey	grave 106	H1 c20.0	-	knife	-	*Surrey Arch.Collections*, LVI, 1959, 66, 123.
Mitcham Surrey	grave 113	E2 c25.0	-	knife, shield	-	*Surrey Arch.Collections*, LVI, 1959, 67, 123.
		E2 c25.0	-		-	*Surrey Arch.Collectoons*, LVI, 1959, 67, 123.
Mitcham Surrey	grave 125	G2 35.9f	-	shield	Cambridge Museum 58.5	*Surrey Arch.Collections*, LVI, 1959, 69, 123.
Mitcham Surrey	grave 207	H3 31.4	-	-	London Museum A.19859	*Surrey Arch.Collections*, LVI, 1959, 73, 123.
Mitcham Surrey	grave 211	H2 c23.0	-	sword, shield	-	*Surrey Arch.Collections*, LVI, 1959, 74, 123.
Mitcham Surrey	grave 213	K1 8.7	-	knife, shield	London Museum A.20035	*Surrey Arch.Collections*, LVI, 1959, 74, 123.
Mitcham Surrey	grave 223	H1 13.3	-	knife	London Museum A.20289	*Surrey Arch.Collections*, LVI, 1959, 74, 123.
Mitcham Surrey	grave 228	H2 26.9	-	-	London Museum A.24433	*Surrey Arch.Collections*, LVI, 1959, 75, 123.
Mitcham Surrey	grave G	E3 34.4	-	-	Kingston Museum L.36	*Surrey Arch.Collections*, LVI, 1959, 124.
Mitcham Surrey	grave H	E3 f36.0g	-	-	Kingston Museum L.37	*Surrey Arch.Collections*, LVI, 1959, 124.
Mitcham Surrey	grave I	G2 43.0	-	-	Kingston Museum L.38	-
Mitcham Surrey	grave	H2 18.3f	-	-	Cambridge Museum 58.6	*Surrey Arch.Collections*, LVI, 1959, 124.
Mitcham Surrey	grave	G2 f)34.3	-	-	Cambridge Museum 58.18	-
Mitcham Surrey	grave	F2 f30.0	-	-	Cambridge Museum 58.19	-
Mitcham Surrey	grave	H2 27.2	-	-	Cambridge Museum 58.20	-
Mitcham Surrey	grave	E1 f)17.8	-	-	Cambridge Museum 58.21	-
Mitcham Surrey	grave	E1 11.9	-	-	Cambridge Museum 58.22	-
Mitcham Surrey	grave	H1 16.5	-	-	Kingston Museum L.27	-
Mitcham Surrey	grave	E2 f17.1	-	-	Kingston Museum L.28	-
Mitcham Surrey	grave	J 15.3	-	-	Kingston Museum L.29	-
Mitcham Surrey	grave	H1 f)16.7	-	-	Kingston Museum L.30	-
Mitcham Surrey	grave	C1 f)10.4(f	-	-	Kingston Museum L.31	-

Provenance	Nature of find.	Type Length	Butt-ferrule	Associated weapons.	Museum Accession no.	Publication
Mitcham Surrey	grave	H2 27.4	-	-	Kingston Museum L.32	-
Mitcham Surrey	grave	H2 25.1	-	-	Kingston Museum L.33	-
Mitcham Surrey	grave	H2 24.6	-	-	Kingston Museum L.34	-
Mitcham Surrey	grave	C2 25.8	-	-	Kingston Museum L.35	-
Mitcham Surrey	grave	G1 30.0	-	-	London Museum 56.106.7	-
Mitcham Surrey	grave	E4 f28.7(f	-	-	London Museum 56.106.10	-
Mitcham Surrey	grave	H2 26.0	-	-	London Museum 56.106.12	-
Mitcham Surrey	grave	E4 f)23.4	-	-	London Museum C.2445	-
Mitcham Surrey	grave	H2 22.1	-	-	London Museum	-
Mitchell's Hill Suffolk	grave	E3 40.2f	-	-	British Museum 1932 10-10 1	-
Mitchell's Hill Suffolk	grave	H3 f28.0	-	-	British Museum 1932 10-10 2	-
Monsal Dale Derbs.	-	C2 22.0(f	-	-	Sheffield Museum J.93.695	*Ten Years' Digging*, 74.
Mortlake Surrey	River Thames	D1 f24.9	-	-	British Museum 1906 7-2 5	-
Mortlake Surrey	River Thames	F2 21.9	-	-	London Museum A.13934	*London & the Saxons*, 163, pl.ix,6.
Mortlake Surrey	River Thames	H2 24.7	-	-	London Museum A.13998	-
Mortlake Surrey	River Thames	I2 33.0	-	-	London Museum A.14651	*London & the Saxons*, 168, pl.x,7.
Mortlake Surrey	River Thames	J 18.0f	-	-	London Museum A.15463	*London & the Saxons*, 168, fig.39,6.
Mortlake Surrey	River Thames	D2 20.0	-	-	Toronto Museum 927.66.1	-
Mortlake Surrey	River Thames	J 20.6	-	-	Toronto Museum 927.66.2	-
Mucking Essex	grave 159	C3 27.0	-	-	-	-
Mucking Essex	grave 243	H1 19.0	-	-	-	-
Mucking Essex	grave 244	K1 19.0	-	-	-	*Spearheads*, 213.
Mucking Essex	grave 245	H2 28.0	-	-	-	-
Mucking Essex	grave 248	H2 31.5	conical	-	-	-
Mucking Essex	grave 260	H2 34.4	-	-	-	-
Mucking Essex	grave 276	C1 16.5	-	-	-	-
Mucking Essex	grave 286	C3 33.0	-	-	-	-
Mucking Essex	grave 338	C2 20.0	-	-	-	-
Mucking Essex	grave 343	E1 17.3	-	-	-	-
Mucking Essex	grave 350	C2 29.5	-	-	-	-
Mucking Essex	grave 493	E1 f)19.3	-	knife	-	*Spearheads*, 177.
Narford Norfolk	grave	F2 f)45.1	-	shield	Kings Lynn Museum A.101	*Antiqu.Journal*, XLIII, 1963, 41, fig. 13g.
Nassington Northants.	grave 23	H2 24.3	-	knife	Peterborough Museum	*Antiqu.Journal*, XXIV, 1944, 108.

Provenance	Nature of find.	Type Length	Butt-ferrule	Associated weapons.	Museum Accession no.	Publication
Nassington Northants.	grave 25	F2 24.3	-	knife, shield	Peterborough Museum	*Antiqu.Journal*, XXIV, 1944, 108, fig.4.
Nassington Northants.	grave 26	H3 32.4	-	knife	Peterborough Museum	*Antiqu.Journal*, XXIV, 1944, 109.
Nassington Northants.	grave 27b	G2 26.9	-	2 knives, shield	Peterborough Museum	*Antiqu.Journal*, XXIV, 1944, 109.
Nassington Northants.	grave 37	H2 29.7	-	knife	Peterborough Museum	*Antiqu.Journal*, XXIV, 1944, 111.
Nassington Northants.	grave 42	H3 35.0	-	-	Peterborough Museum	*Antiqu.Journal*, XXIV, 1944, 111.
Nassington Northants.	grave	L 38.2	-	-	Oundle School	*Antiqu.Journal*, XXIV, 1944, 114, fig.4, pl.xxix.
Nassington Northants.	grave	E4 f21.3	-	-	Peterborough Museum	-
Nassington Northants.	grave	J 32.0	-	-	Peterborough Museum	-
Nassington Northants.	grave	H3 f)31.8	-	-	Peterborough Museum	-
Netheravon Wilts.	grave	H1 f13.2f	-	shield	Devizes Museum 95	*Wilts.Arch.Magazine*, XLVIII, 1938, 469-70.
Nethercourt Farm, Kent	grave	C3 f)41.2(f	-	knife, seax	-	*Arch.Cantiana*, LXIX, 1955, 202, pl.i.
Nether Wallop Hants.	-	E2 35.1	-	-	Salisbury Museum	*Proc.Hants.Field Club*, XII, 1934, 208.
Northampton III Northants.	grave	H2 26.2	-	-	Northampton Museum D.231	-
Northfleet Kent	grave 1	C3 37.9	conical	-	-	*JBAA.*, III, 1848, 236, fig. 3.
Northfleet Kent	grave 2	C1 15.2	-	-	-	*JBAA.*, III, 1848, 236, fig. 4.
Northfleet Kent	grave	E1 16.7	-	-	Gravesend Museum	-
Northfleet Kent	grave	A2 f56.0	-	-	Gravesend Museum	-
Northfleet Kent	grave	E3 f38.8f	-	-	Gravesend Museum	-
Northfleet Kent	grave	H2 22.0f	-	-	Gravesend Museum	-
Northfleet Kent	grave	C2 f)23.5	-	-	Gravesend Museum	-
Northfleet Kent	grave	H1 f)20.1(f	-	-	Maidstone Museum	-
Northfleet Kent	grave	H1 22.2	-	-	Maidstone Museum	-
Northfleet Kent	grave	H1 20.3(f	-	-	Maidstone Museum	-
Northfleet Kent	grave	H2 23.4	-	-	Maidstone Museum	-
Northfleet Kent	grave	H1 22.1	-	-	Maidstone Museum	-
Northfleet Kent	grave	H1 f)17.5f	-	-	Maidstone Museum	-
Northfleet Kent	grave	H2 f)23.0	-	-	Maidstone Museum	-
Northfleet Kent	grave	E4 f)26.0f	-	-	Maidstone Museum	-
Northfleet Kent	grave	E2 f16.8(f	-	-	Maidstone Museum	-
North Luffenham Rutland	grave 1	H2 26.5	conical 7.7	knife, sword, shield	-	*Rutland Magazine*, I, 1904, 90, pl.i.
North Luffenham Rutland	grave 2	F3 26.5	-	knife, sword, shield	-	*Rutland Magazine*, I, 1904, 90, pl.1.
North Luffenham Rutland	grave	C4 41.8f	-	-	Leicester Museum 1 1946	-
North Luffenham Rutland	grave	E1 17.4	-	-	Oakham School	-

Provenance	Nature of find.	Type Length	Butt-ferrule	Associated weapons.	Museum Accession no.	Publication
North Luffenham Rutland	grave	H3 33.1(f	-	-	Oakham School	-
North Luffenham Rutland	grave	F3 f)29.4f	-	-	Oakham School	-
North Luffenham Rutland	grave	C4 31.3f	-	-	Oakham School	-
North Suffolk	-	F3 24.9	-	-	Bury St Edmunds Museum L.34	-
Norwich Norfolk	-	E3 f)31.9f	-	-	Norwich Museum 214.949	-
Oddington Glos.	grave	F2 16.5	-	-	-	Gentleman's Magazine, LVII, 1787, 292, fig.4.
Oddington Glos.	grave	E3 21.5	-	-	-	Gentleman's Magazine, LVII, 1787, 292, fig.5.
Odstock Wilts.	-	C1 f)9.6f	-	-	Salisbury Museum	
Old Shifford Oxon.	River Thames	E4 38.2	-	-	Ashmolean Museum 1914 83	-
Old Shifford Oxon.	River Thames	H1 18.0	-	-	Ashmolean Museum 1914 84	-
Old Windsor Berks.	River Thames	F2 f)29.0	-	-	Toronto Museum 910.153.5	-
Oliver's Battery Hants.	grave	C2 f16.5	*	seax	British Museum	Proc.Hants.Field Club, XII, 1934, 12, 16, fig.iv.
Orpington Kent	grave 3	H2 31.2	-	knife, shield	Orpington Museum	Arch.Cantiana, LXXXIII, 1968, 131, fig.10.
Orpington Kent	grave 5	C2 f)32.7	-	knife, shield	Orpington Museum	Arch.Cantiana, LXXXIII, 1968, 132, fig.10.
Orpington Kent	grave 25	C2 f)22.4	-	knife, shield	Orpington Museum	Arch.Cantiana, LXXXIII, 1968, 138, fig.10.
Orpington Kent	grave 26	H3 33.8(f	-	knife, shield	Orpington Museum	Arch.Cantiana, LXXXIII, 1968, 138, fig.10.
Orpington Kent	grave 37	H2 22.5	-	knife, shield	Orpington Museum	Arch.Cantiana, LXXXIII, 1968, 143, fig.10.
Orpington Kent	grave 38	H2 27.4	-	knife, shield	Orpington Museum	Arch.Cantiana, LXXXIII, 1968, 143, fig.10.
Orpington Kent	grave 42	H3 34.0	-	shield	Orpington Museum	Arch.Cantiana, LXXXIII, 1968, 145, fig.10.
Orpington Kent	grave 71	H2 22.8	-	-	Orpington Museum	Arch.Cantiana, LXXXIV, 1969, 49, fig.2.
Orpington Kent	?grave	C1 f)16.8	-	-	Orpington Museum	Arch.Cantiana, LXXXIV, 1969, 50, fig.2.
Osengal Kent	grave 1	E3 27.8			Ramsgate Public Library	Arch.Cantiana, LXXXIV, 1969, 14-5, fig.2.
Osengal Kent	grave 3	H3 f)41.2	-	-	Ramsgate Public Library	Arch.Cantiana, LXXXIV, 1969, 15, fig.2.
Osengal Kent	grave	H3 49.8	-	-	Ramsgate Public Library	Arch.Cantiana, LXXXIV, 1969, 15, fig.2.
Osengal Kent	grave	E2 21.9	-	-	-	Collectanea Antiqua, III, pl. i,11.
Osengal Kent	grave	C2 23.7	-	-	-	Collectanea Antiqua, III, pl. i,12.
Osengal Kent	grave	C2 26.4	-	-	-	Collectanea Antiqua, III, pl. i,13.
Osengal Kent	grave	E3 29.4	-	-	-	Collectanea Antiqua, III, pl. i,14.
Osengal Kent	grave	C2 30.3	-	-	-	Collectanea Antiqua, III, pl. i,15.
Osengal Kent	grave	C3 32.1	-	-	-	Collectanea Antiqua, III, pl. i,16.
Osengal Kent	grave	C2 31.2	-	-	-	Collectanea Antiqua, III, pl. i,17.
Osengal Kent	grave	C3 37.2	-	-	-	Collectanea Antiqua, III, 6, pl. i,18.
Osengal Kent	grave	H3 37.5	-	-	-	Collectanea Antiqua, III, pl. i,19.

Provenance	Nature of find.	Type Length	Butt-ferrule	Associated weapons.	Museum Accession no.	Publication
Osengal Kent	grave	H3 48.5	-	-	-	*Collectanea Antiqua*, III, pl. i,20.
Osengal Kent	grave	C2 37.5	-	-	-	*Collectanea Antiqua*, III, pl. i,21.
Osengal Kent	grave	H3 38.4	-	-	-	*Collectanea Antiqua*, III, pl. i,22.
Osengal Kent	grave	C3 40.8	-	-	-	*Collectanea Antiqua*, III, pl. i,23.
Osengal Kent	grave	C2 41.4	-	-	-	*Collectanea Antiqua*, III, pl. i,24.
Osengal Kent	grave	H3 51.3	-	-	-	*Collectanea Antiqua*, III, pl. i,25.
Out Elmstead Kent	grave	K1 28.9	-	-	private collection	*British Numismatic Journal*, XXX, 1960-1, 8.
Oxford Oxon.	grave	H1 f)18.9	-	-	Ashmolean Museum 1883 197	-
Oxford Oxon.	grave	H2 21.4	-	-	Ashmolean Museum 1883 197	-
Oxford Oxon.	surface find	F2 48.8	-	-	Ashmolean Museum 1957 70	*Oxoniensia*, XXIII, 1958, 137, fig. 43.
Oxford Oxon.	River Thames	E2 22.8	-	-	-	*Berks.Buck.& Oxon.Arch. Journal*, IV, 1898, 25.
Pangbourne Berks.	-	B2 58.9	-	-	British Museum CRS. collection	*Collectanea Antiqua*, II, 224.
Partney Lincs.	grave 1	L 38.3	-	-	Lincoln Museum 49.50	*Antiqu.Journal*, XXXIV, 1954, 229, pl.xx.
Partney Lincs.	grave 2	H2 f)21.3	-	-	Lincoln Museum 48.50	*Antiqu.Journal*, XXXIV, 1954, 229, pl.xx.
Partney Lincs.	grave 3	E4 f16.0f	-	-	Lincoln Museum	*Antiqu.Journal*, XXXIV, 1954, 229, pl.xx.
Pebworth Down Worcs.	grave	C5 26.0	-	-	Warwick Museum 155 1957	-
Perham Down Wilts.	grave	E3 30.1	-	shield	Salisbury Museum	*Wilts.Arch.Magazine*, XLIX, 1942, 114.
Peterborough I Northants.	grave	C2 f)21.0	-	-	Peterborough Museum L.547	-
Peterborough I Northants.	grave	H2 22.5	-	-	Peterborough Museum L.548	-
Peterborough I Northants.	grave	H2 24.7	-	-	Peterborough Museum L.549	-
Peterborough I Northants.	grave	H3 f)31.7	-	-	Peterborough Museum L.550	-
Peterborough I Northants.	grave	H2 27.3	-	-	Peterborough Museum L.551	-
Peterborough I Northants.	grave	C2 f)34.4f	-	-	Peterborough Museum L.552	-
Peterborough I Northants.	grave	E2 31.2	-	-	Peterborough Museum L.553	*Spearheads*, fig. 25d.
Peterborough I Northants.	grave	H2 29.5	-	-	Peterborough Museum L.554	-
Peterborough I Northants.	grave	H2 f)23.2f	-	-	Peterborough Museum L.555	-
Peterborough I Northants.	grave	F1 f)19.8	-	-	Peterborough Museum L.556	*Spearheads*, fig. 31c.
Peterborough I Northants.	grave	D1 21.8	-	-	Peterborough Museum L.557	-
Peterborough I Northants.	grave	E4 f40.9(f	-	-	Peterborough Museum L.559-60	-
Peterborough I Northants.	grave	E3 f)36.9	-	-	Peterborough Museum L.561	-
Peterborough I Northants.	grave	C3 55.6(f	-	-	Peterborough Museum L.563	-
Peterborough I Northants.	grave	G1 22.9	-	-	Peterborough Museum	-
Peterborough I Northants.	grave	H2 f)28.5	-	-	Peterborough Museum	-

Provenance	Nature of find.	Type Length	Butt-ferrule	Associated weapons.	Museum Accession no.	Publication
Peterborough I Northants.	grave	E3 34.1	-	-	Peterborough Museum	-
Petersfinger Wilts.	grave 3	H1 15.9	-	shield	Salisbury Museum	*Petersfinger*, 6, fig. 6,7.
Petersfinger Wilts.	grave 6	I1 f)17.4	-	knife	Salisbury Museum	*Petersfinger*, 8, fig. 6,10.
Petersfinger Wilts.	grave 7	C2 f)23.1	-	sword, shield	Salisbury Museum	*Petersfinger*, 8, fig. 6,14.
Petersfinger Wilts.	grave 11a	H2 26.6	-	knife, shield	Salisbury Museum	*Petersfinger*, 10, fig. 6,29.
Petersfinger Wilts.	grave 20	C3 41.1	conical 7.5	sword, shield	Salisbury Museum	*Petersfinger*, 13, fig. 6,48-9, pl.ii,48.
Petersfinger Wilts.	grave 21	H1 f)17.5	stud diam. 2.2	knife, sword, axe	Salisbury Museum	*Petersfinger*, 16, fig. 6,59.
Petersfinger Wilts.	grave 27	L f)19.5	-	knife, shield	Salisbury Museum	*Petersfinger*, 24, fig. 6,98.
Petersfinger Wilts.	grave 31	C1 c16.0	-	-	-	*Petersfinger*, 26.
Petersfinger Wilts.	grave 33	C4 43.3	-	knife	Salisbury Museum	*Petersfinger*, 26, fig. 7,116.
Petersfinger Wilts.	grave 55	K1 f)25.5	conical 5.2	knife	Salisbury Museum	*Petersfinger*, 36, fig. 7,147.
Petersfinger Wilts.	grave 58	H1 22.5	-	knife, shield	Salisbury Museum	*Petersfinger*, 37, fig. 7,156.
Petersfinger Wilts.	grave 59	H1 20.6	-	-	Salisbury Museum	*Petersfinger*, 38, fig. 7,161.
Petersfinger Wilts.	grave 60	H2 28.5	conical 5.9f	knife, shield	Salisbury Museum	*Petersfinger*, 40, fig. 7,163.
Petersfinger Wilts.	grave 61b	H2 f)22.6	-	knife	Salisbury Museum	*Petersfinger*, 41, fig. 7,170.
Pewsey Wilts.	grave 5	H1 13.7	-	knife, shield	Devizes Museum	-
Pewsey Wilts.	grave 8	L 20.1	conical 7.4	shield	Devizes Museum	*Spearheads*, 137, fig.53a.
Pewsey Wilts.	grave 12	H2 29.3	conical 6.9	-	Devizes Museum	*Spearheads*, 201.
Pewsey Wilts.	grave 16	E1 7.8	-	-	Devizes Museum	-
Pewsey Wilts.	grave 22	H3 58.0(f	conical 9.8	knife, sword, shield	Devizes Museum	*Spearheads*, 205.
Pewsey Wilts.	grave 28	H1 21.3	-	-	Devizes Museum	-
Pitstone Bucks.	grave	C2 53.2	-	-	Luton Museum 291.61	-
Pittington Durham	surface find	E1 11.6f	-	-	Newcastle Museum	*Trans.A.S.Northumberland & Durham*, IX, 1939, 139, pl.
Polhill Kent	grave 27	F2 f)36.5	-	knife	-	*West Kent*, 175, fig.59,602.
Polhill Kent	grave 40	C5 f)16.8	-	knife	-	*West Kent*, 177, fig.59,603.
Polhill Kent	grave 45	D1 20.4	-	knife	-	*West Kent*, 177, fig.59,604.
Polhill Kent	grave 65	C2 25.8	-	knife	-	*West Kent*, 180, fig.59,605.
Polhill Kent	grave 68	D1 28.0	-	knife	-	*West Kent*, 180, fig.59,607.
Polhill Kent	grave 68	D2 15.3f	-	knife	-	*West Kent*, 180, fig.59,606.
Polhill Kent	grave 69	F2 31.8	-	knife	-	*West Kent*, 180, fig.59,608.
Polhill Kent	grave 73	C3 f27.3f	-	knife	-	*West Kent*, 181, fig.59,609.
Polhill Kent	grave 81	C2 27.9	-	knife	-	*West Kent*, 182, fig.59,610.
Polhill Kent	grave 84	C5 24.9	-	2 knives, seax	-	*West Kent*, 182, fig.59,611.

Provenance	Nature of find	Type Length	Butt-ferrule	Associated weapons	Museum Accession no.	Publication
Polhill Kent	grave 85	C5 f)26.4	-	knife, seax	-	*West Kent,* 182, fig.59,612.
Polhill Kent	grave 97	C2 f)31.7	-	-	-	*West Kent,* 184, fig.59,613.
Polhill Kent	grave 102	C5 25.2	-	knife	-	*West Kent,* 185, fig.59,614.
Portslade Sussex	grave	H3 28.6f	-	knife, shield	Hove Museum 80 1931	*Sussex Notes & Queries,* III, 1931, 214, pl.
Prittlewell Essex	grave A	E3 40.3	-	-	British Museum 92 11-4 16	*Spearheads,* fig. 27d.
Prittlewell Essex	grave 2	D2 48.4	-	knife	Southend Museum 159.23	*Trans.Southend Ant.Soc.,* I, 1923, 116, pl.
Prittlewell Essex	grave 3	E3 f)36.4(f	*	knife	Southend Museum 159.25	*Trans.Southend Ant.Soc.,* I, 1923, 116, pl.
Prittlewell Essex	grave 6	C3 22.0f	-	2 knives, shield	Southend Museum 159.29	*Trans.Southend Ant.Soc.,* I, 1923, 118, pl.
Prittlewell Essex	grave 8	E3 36.6	-	-	-	*Trans.Southend Ant.Soc.,* I, 1923, 118, pl.
Prittlewell Essex	grave 18	C3 24.4	-	sword, shield	Southend Museum 159.6	*Trans.Southend Ant.Soc.,* I, 1923, 121, pl.
Prittlewell Essex	grave 22	D3 25.2	-	another spear	Southend Museum 159.22	*Trans.Southend Ant.Soc.,* I, 1923, 121, pl.
Prittlewell Essex	grave 23	F3 34.1	-	-	Southend Museum 159.54	*Trans.Southend Ant.Soc.,* I, 1923, 121, pl.
Prittlewell Essex	grave 25	E3 f36.6	-	sword, shield	Southend Museum 179.3	*Trans.Southend Ant.Soc.,* I, 1923, 122, pl.
Prittlewell Essex	grave 26	C2 18.4	-	-	Southend Museum 179.5	*Trans.Southend Ant.Soc.,* I, 1923, 122, pl.
Prittlewell Essex	grave 27	E4 41.7f	-	knife, shield	Southend Museum 179.4	*Trans.Southend Ant.Soc.,* I, 1923, 122, pl.
Prittlewell Essex	grave 28	C2 21.5	-	-	Southend Museum 159.56	*Trans.Southend Ant.Soc.,* I, 1923, 122, pl.
Prittlewell Essex	grave 29	G2 f)35.2	-	-	Southend Museum 159.57	*Trans.Southend Ant.Soc.,* I, 1923, 122, pl.
Prittlewell Essex	grave 30	H1 18.4f	-	-	Southend Museum 159.58	*Trans.Southend Ant.Soc.,* I, 1923, 122, pl.
Prittlewell Essex	grave	C2 f)16.4f	-	-	Southend Museum 159.27	-
Prittlewell Essex	grave	E3 37.5	-	-	Southend Museum 159.36	-
Prittlewell Essex	grave	E3 f)34.6f	-	-	Southend Museum 425.2	-
Prittlewell Essex	grave	E4 f25.8	-	-	Southend Museum 425.3	-
Prittlewell Essex	grave	D2 20.1f	-	-	Southend Museum 425.4	-
Prittlewell Essex	grave	C2 f36.4f	-	-	Southend Museum 438.2	-
Purton Wilts.	grave	H2 29.9	-	-	Ashmolean Museum	*Wilts.Arch.Magazine,* XXXVII, 1912, 608, fig.
Purton Wilts.	grave	C2 24.9	-	seax	Devizes Museum 80	*Wilts.Arch.Magazine,* XXXVII, 1912, 608, fig.
Putney London	River Thames	L f)19.7f	-	-	British Museum	-
Putney London	River Thames	H1 19.5	-	-	London Museum A.11911	*London & the Saxons,* 163, pl. ix,2.
Putney London	River Thames	G1 f)24.7	-	-	London Museum A.24940	-
Putney London	River Thames	I2 27.4	-	-	London Museum A.24938	*London & the Saxons,* 168, pl. x,5.
Puxton Worcs.	-	G2 f52.4	-	-	Kidderminster Museum 49 1960	*Spearheads,* fig. 35c.
Rainham Essex	grave	E2 f23.0	-	-	Dagenham Museum	*Archaeologia,* XCVI, 1955, 169, pl. lix.
Rainham Essex	grave	C3 f36.5f	-	-	Dagenham Museum	*Archaeologia,* XCVI, 1955, 169, pl. lix.

Provenance	Nature of find.	Type Length	Butt-ferrule	Associated weapons.	Museum Accession no.	Publication
Rainham Essex	grave	E2 21.3	-	-	Dagenham Museum	Archaeologia, XCVI, 1955, 169, pl. lix.
Rainham Essex	grave	H2 21.5(f	-	-	Dagenham Museum	Archaeologia, XCVI, 1955, 169, pl. lix.
Ranworth Norfolk	-	E3 51.7	-	-	Norwich Museum 11.398	Norfolk Archaeology, XXVII, 1939, 239.
Reading I Berks.	grave 3	H2 23.7	-	knife	Reading Museum	JBAA., L, 1894, 151, fig. 1.
Reading I Berks.	grave 12	H2 19.2	-	-	Reading Museum	JBAA., L, 1894, 153, fig. 21.
Reading I Berks.	surface find	K2 20.9	-	-	Reading Museum 2.38	-
Reading Berks.	River Thames	H3 33.1f	-	-	Reading Museum 24.40	-
Reading Berks.	River Kennet	E4 f32.7f	-	-	Reading Museum 238.62	-
Reading Berks.	River Kennet	E2 19.7f	-	-	Reading Museum	-
Readon Hill Staffs.	grave	C3 f14.1f	-	knife	Sheffield Museum J.93.1152	Ten Years' Digging, 122.
Redbourne Herts.	?grave	H3 f)33.7f	-	-	St Albans Museum	-
Richborough Castle, Kent	grave	B2 22.0	-	sword, shield	site museum	Richborough IV, 155, fig., pl. lxiii.
Richborough Castle, Kent	Roman fort	B2 16.4f	-	-	site museum	Richborough IV, 153, pl. lviii,286.
Richborough Castle, Kent	Roman fort	C2 f)25.8	-	-	site museum	Richborough IV, 153, pl. lviii,278.
Richborough Castle, Kent	Roman fort	C2 f)15.4(f	-	-	site museum	Richborough IV, 153, pl. lviii,285.
Richborough Castle, Kent	Roman fort	C2 24.4	-	-	site museum	Richborough V, 108.
Ripley Surrey	surface find	L 23.6(f	-	-	-	Surrey Arch.Collections, LII, 1950, 82, fig.2.
Riseley Kent	grave 21	H2 30.2	-	-	Dartford Museum	Trans.Dartford Ant.Soc., VIII, 1938, 17.
Riseley Kent	grave 66	H2 f)21.8	-	knife, shield, ?another spear	Dartford Museum	Trans.Dartford Ant.Soc., VIII, 1938, 20.
Riseley Kent	grave 70	H1 18.5	-	knife	Dartford Museum	Trans.Dartford Ant.Soc., VIII, 1938, 21.
Riseley Kent	grave 76	E4 41.6	-	knife	Dartford Museum	Trans.Dartford Ant.Soc., VIII, 1938, 22.
Riseley Kent	grave 86	K1 f)11.6f	-	knife, sword shield	Dartford Museum	Trans.Dartford Ant.Soc., VIII, 1938, 24.
Riseley Kent	grave	C2 28.7	-	-	Dartford Museum	-
Riseley Kent	grave	C2 28.4	-	-	Dartford Museum	-
Riseley Kent	grave	H2 30.3	-	-	Dartford Museum	-
Rochester II Kent	grave	C2 f)20.6f	-	-	Rochester Museum X.4	-
Rochester II Kent	grave	H3 f)32.2f	-	-	Rochester Museum X.9	-
Rochester II Kent	grave	B2 26.7f	-	-	Rochester Museum X.10	Spearheads, 41, fig. 7e.
Rochester II Kent	grave	H3 f35.4f	-	-	Rochester Museum X.114	-
Rochester II Kent	grave	F2 f)31.2	-	-	Rochester Museum X.115	-
Rochester II Kent	grave	H3 f26.1f	-	-	Rochester Museum X.116	-
Rochester II Kent	grave	H1 19.9	-	-	Rochester Museum X.117	-
Rochester II Kent	grave	H1 f21.3f	-	-	Rochester Museum X.118	-

Provenance	Nature of find.	Type Length	Butt-ferrule	Associated weapons.	Museum Accession no.	Publication
Romsey Hants.	-	F2 f)49.0	-	-	Romsey Abbey	-
Rothley Temple Leics.	?grave	H3 f27.7	-	-	Leicester Museum 14.IL 1953	-
Rothley Temple Leics.	?grave	C2 28.4	-	-	Leicester Museum 26 1901	-
Rothley Temple Leics.	?grave	C3 38.7	-	-	Leicester Museum 116 1962 208a	-
Rothley Temple Leics.	?grave	E4 f29.9	-	-	Leicester Museum 116 1962 208b	-
Roundway Down Wilts.	surface find	E4 48.6	-	-	Devizes Museum 8.58.317	-
Rowley Fields Leics.	?grave	E2 f)18.2(f	-	-	Leicester Museum 47 1940	-
Ruskington Lincs.	grave	E3 44.6	-	-	Grantham Museum AS.84	*Antiqu.Journal*, XXXVI, 1956, 181.
Ruskington Lincs.	grave	H2 24.8	-	-	Grantham Museum AS.84	*Antiqu.Journal*, XXXVI, 1956, 181.
Ruskington Lincs.	grave	D3 18.7	-	-	Lincoln Museum 15-40.38a	*Spearheads*, fig. 21c.
Ruskington Lincs.	grave	H1 16.0	-	-	Lincoln Museum 15-40.38b	-
Ruskington Lincs.	grave	H3 36.8	-	-	Lincoln Museum 35-56	*Spearheads*, fig. 41d.
Ruskington Lincs.	grave	K2 f17.0	-	-	Lincoln Museum 35-56	-
Ruskington Lincs.	grave	H2 23.6	-	-	Lincoln Museum 35-56	-
Saffron Walden Essex	grave	C3	-	-	-	*Trans.Essex Arch.Soc.*, NS. II, 1884, 311, pl.v,12.
St Albans Herts.	grave SZ3	C2 25.3	-	knife	-	*Spearheads*, 160.
St Albans Herts.	grave SK6	C2 22.8	-	knife	-	*Spearheads*, 160.
St Albans Herts.	grave SY8	C4 33.3	-	knife, seax	-	*Spearheads*, 167.
St Albans Herts.	grave SY16	D1 14.0	-	-	-	-
St Peters Kent	grave 2	E2 f)26.6	-	knife	-	-
St Peters Kent	grave 8	C4 33.2	-	knife	-	*Spearheads*, 167.
St Peters Kent	grave 9	F1 f)30.2	-	knife	-	-
St Peters Kent	grave 12	F2 f)29.2	-	-	-	-
St Peters Kent	grave 23	C2 f15.2	-	knife, seax	-	*Spearheads*, 160.
St Peters Kent	grave 39	C2 28.6	-	knife	-	-
St Peters Kent	grave 42	D2 18.9f	-	2 knives	-	-
St Peters Kent	grave 45	C2 f27.2	-	knife	-	*Spearheads*, 160.
St Peters Kent	grave 50	D2 f25.8	conical 7.6(f	knife	-	-
St Peters Kent	grave 53	E3 36.6f	-	knife	-	-
St Peters Kent	grave 54	C2 34.0 / D2 f)27.2	conical 8.2 / -	knife, sword, shield	-	-
St Peters Kent	grave 58	F2 27.2f	-	knife	-	-
St Peters Kent	grave 68	F3 35.6	-	knife, sword, shield	-	-

Provenance	Nature of find.	Type Length	Butt-ferrule	Associated weapons.	Museum Accession no.	Publication
St Peters Kent	grave 74	D2 24.0	-	knife	-	-
		D3 27.8	-		-	-
St Peters Kent	grave 97	C3 41.0(f	-	knife	-	-
St Peters Kent	grave 167	B1 15.2f	-	knife	-	-
St Peters Kent	grave 173	H3 f36.6	-	-	-	-
St Peters Kent	grave 178	D2 14.2	-	2 knives	-	-
St Peters Kent	grave 190	C3 35.6f	conical 8.0	knife	-	-
St Peters Kent	grave 192	D2 24.0f	-	knife	-	*Spearheads*, 175.
St Peters Kent	grave 194	C2 27.8	-	knife	-	-
St Peters Kent	grave 196	C2 30.2	-	knife, sword, shield	-	-
St Peters Kent	grave 197	D2 22.0	-	-	-	-
St Peters Kent	grave 198	E3 46.6	-	knife	-	-
St Peters Kent	grave 200	E2 f)23.3f	conical 5.4	knife, shield	-	-
St Peters Kent	grave 202	C3 36.2	-	knife	-	-
St Peters Kent	grave 203	C2 23.8	*	knife	-	-
St Peters Kent	grave 206	C1 16.6	-,	knife	-	-
St Peters Kent	grave 212	E3 35.2	-	knife	-	-
St Peters Kent	grave 214	F3 30.6	-	-	-	-
St Peters Kent	grave 218	C2 24.2	-	knife, shield	-	-
St Peters Kent	grave 223	C4 20.9	-	knife	-	-
St Peters Kent	grave 227	F3 33.4	-	knife, shield	-	*Spearheads*, 189.
St Peters Kent	grave 249	H3 f)49.4	-	knife	-	-
St Peters Kent	grave 250	H3 40.2	-	knife, shield	-	*Spearheads*, 205.
St Peters Kent	grave 254	C4 f28.5	-	knife, shield	-	-
St Peters Kent	grave 255	C3 31.2	-	knife, shield	-	-
St Peters Kent	grave 263	E3 34.0	-	knife	-	*Spearheads*, 181.
St Peters Kent	grave 267	F2 f25.4	-	knife, shield	-	*Spearheads*, 185.
St Peters Kent	grave 270	D2 24.0	-	knife, shield	-	-
		E2 43.2	conical 3.2		-	-
St Peters Kent	grave 288	C2 20.9(f	-	knife, sword, shield	-	-
St Peters Kent	grave 289	D2 32.8	-	knife, sword, shield	-	*Spearheads*, 175.
St Peters Kent	grave 292	E2 22.2	-	knife, shield	-	-
St Peters Kent	grave 295	C3 f37.2	-	knife	-	-

Provenance	Nature of find.	Type Length	Butt-ferrule	Associated weapons.	Museum Accession no.	Publication
St Peters Kent	grave 304	C4 26.6	-	knife, sword	-	-
St Peters Kent	grave 307b	C2 23.2	-	knife	-	-
St Peters Kent	grave 308	E4 34.2	-	knife	-	*Spearheads*, 183.
St Peters Kent	grave 309	D2 22.5	-	knife	-	*Spearheads*, 175.
St Peters Kent	grave 313	F2 18.2	-	knife	-	*Spearheads*, 185.
St Peters Kent	grave 315	F2 33.0	-	knife, sword, shield	-	*Spearheads*, 185.
St Peters Kent	grave 318	D2 29.0	*	knife	-	-
St Peters Kent	grave 325	B1 15.2	-	knife	-	-
St Peters Kent	grave 334	C2 32.0	-	knife, shield	-	*Spearheads*, 160.
St Peters Kent	grave 355	D2 30.2	-	knife	-	-
St Peters Kent	grave 356	E3 44.9	-	knife, sword, shield	-	-
St Peters Kent	grave 357	D1 28.9	-	knife	-	-
St Peters Kent	grave 358	E3 f30.2	-	knife	-	*Spearheads*, 181.
St Peters Kent	grave 359	F2 34.0	conical 8.2	knife	-	-
St Peters Kent	grave 360	C3 43.0	-	knife	-	-
Salisbury Wilts.	grave	H3 33.5	-	-	Salisbury Museum 1772.98.50	*Wilts.Arch.Magazine*, XLVI, 1934, 155.
Salisbury Wilts.	grave	H3 f24.5f	-	-	Salisbury Museum 1772.98.50	*Wilts.Arch.Magazine*, XLVI, 1934, 155.
Salisbury Wilts.	grave	H2 27.6	-	knife	Salisbury Museum	*Wilts.Arch.Magazine*, XLVI, 1934, 169.
Salisbury Racecourse, Wilts.	grave	C2 f20.5	-	2 knives, sword, shield	-	*Wilts.Arch.Magazine*, XXXVIII, 1914, 236.
		E2 26.1	-		-	*Wilts.Arch.Magazine*, XXXVIII, 1914, 236.
Saltburn-on-Sea Yorks.	grave	C2 f19.5	-	-	Middlesborough Museum	*Yorks.Arch.Journal*, XXII, 1913, 136.
Sancton II Yorks.	grave	C3 49.9	-	-	Hull Museum 156	-
Sarre Kent	grave 3	H2 27.5	*	sword, shield	-	*Arch.Cantiana*, V, 1863, 310; VII, 1868, pl.xiv.
Sarre Kent	grave 10	H2 f18.6	*	knife	-	*Arch.Cantiana*, VI, 1866, 159; VII, 1868, pl.xiv.
Sarre Kent	grave 39a	H3 41.8	*	knife	Maidstone Museum 876	*Arch.Cantiana*, VI, 1866, 165; VII, 1868, pl.xiv.
Sarre Kent	grave 39b	H3 36.6	-	knife, seax, sword, axe, shield, another spear	-	*Arch.Cantiana*, VI, 1866, 165-6.
Sarre Kent	grave 60	H1 20.6	-	knife	Maidstone Museum 918	*Arch.Cantiana*, VI, 1866, 168; VII, 1868, pl.xiii.
Sarre Kent	grave 64	D2 34.6	-	knife, sword, shield	Maidstone Museum 900	*Arch.Cantiana*, VI, 1866, 168; VII, 1868, pl.xiii.
Sarre Kent	grave 89	C2 f)30.2	-	seax, shield	Maidstone Museum	*Arch.Cantiana*, VI, 1866, 172.
		A2 146.0	-		-	*Arch.Cantiana*, VI, 1866, 172; VII, 1868, pl.xiv.
Sarre Kent	grave 135	A2 79.6	-	?knife	-	*Arch.Cantiana*, VI, 1866, 178; VII, 1868, pl.xiv.
Sarre Kent	grave 138	D2 42.2	-	knife	Maidstone Museum 886	*Arch.Cantiana*, VI, 1866, 178; VII, 1868, pl.xiv.
Sarre Kent	grave 142	C2 25.1(f	*	another smaller spear	Maidstone Museum 909	*Arch.Cantiana*, VI, 1866, 178; VII, 1868, pl.xiv.

Provenance	Nature of find.	Type Length	Butt-ferrule	Associated weapons.	Museum Accession no.	Publication
Sarre Kent	grave 153	E3 31.5	-	knife	-	*Arch.Cantiana*, VI, 1866, 179; VII, 1868, pl.xiii.
Sarre Kent	grave 156	E3 40.1	*	sword, shield	Maidstone Museum 889	*Arch.Cantiana*, VI, 1866, 179; VII, 1868, pl.xiii.
Sarre Kent	grave 180	C2 36.4	-	seax	-	*Arch.Cantiana*, VI, 1866, 184.
Sarre Kent	grave 190	C2 24.4f	-	2 knives, sword, shield	Maidstone Museum 916	*Arch.Cantiana*, VII, 1868, 308, pl.xiv.
Sarre Kent	grave 209	C2 f)25.4f	-	knife	Maidstone Museum 899	*Arch.Cantiana*, VII, 1868, 310.
Sarre Kent	grave 211	H2 23.4	-	knife, sword, shield	Maidstone Museum 915	*Arch.Cantiana*, VII, 1868, 311.
Sarre Kent		A2 116.6	-		-	*Arch.Cantiana*, VII, 1868, 311, pl.xiv.
Sarre Kent	grave 253	F3 f31.0(f	-	seax	Maidstone Museum 878	*Arch.Cantiana*, VII, 1868, 315.
Sarre Kent	grave 256	D3 f37.9	*	sword	Maidstone Museum 884	*Arch.Cantiana*, VII, 1868, 316.
Sarre Kent	grave 263	C2 23.6	-	-	-	*Arch.Cantiana*, VII, 1868, 317, pl.xiv.
Sarre Kent	grave	E4 27.9f	-	-	British Museum 93 6-1 212	-
Sarre Kent	grave	G1 f)19.9	-	-	British Museum 93 6-1 213	-
Sarre Kent	grave	E4 38.1	-	-	Maidstone Museum 878	-
Sarre Kent	grave	E4 f39.2f	-	-	Maidstone Museum 881	-
Sarre Kent	grave	E3 25.0f	-	-	Maidstone Museum 895	-
Sarre Kent	grave	F2 31.5(f	-	-	Maidstone Museum 896	-
Sarre Kent	grave	E3 f26.5f	-	-	Maidstone Museum 899	-
Sarre Kent	grave	E3 f24.0	-	-	Maidstone Museum 906	-
Sarre Kent	grave	G1 f)29.3(f	-	-	Maidstone Museum 908	-
Sarre Kent	grave	E4 f28.0f	-	-	Maidstone Museum 911	-
Sarre Kent	grave	E4 f17.4f	-	-	Maidstone Museum 918	-
Sarre Kent	grave	E2 f)23.7f	-	-	Maidstone Museum	-
Sarre Kent	grave	G2 26.4f	-	-	Maidstone Museum	-
Sarre Kent	grave	G2 24.1f	-	-	Maidstone Museum	-
Saxonbury Sussex	grave	C2 31.3	-	-	Lewes Museum 245.1	-
Saxonbury Sussex	grave	K2 f)28.5	-	-	Lewes Museum 245.2	-
Saxonbury Sussex	grave	H3 f)32.4	-	-	Lewes Museum 245.3	-
Saxonbury Sussex	grave	C1 19.0	-	-	Lewes Museum 245.4	-
Scrafield Lincs.	-	I2 f)23.1	-	-	Lincoln Museum 57.38	-
Scunthorpe Lincs.	-	F1 f)23.2	-	-	Scunthorpe Museum	-
Searby Lincs.	grave	G1 26.2	-	-	British Museum 93 6-18 22	*Spearheads*, 189, fig.75g.
Sedgeford Norfolk	-	H3 31.9	-	-	Norwich Museum 187.952	-
Sedgeford Norfolk	-	E4 34.2(f	-	-	Norwich Museum 187.952	*Spearheads*, fig.29b.

Provenance	Nature of find.	Type Length	Butt-ferrule	Associated weapons.	Museum Accession no.	Publication
Selmeston Sussex	grave	E3 f26.5f	–	–	Lewes Museum 52.4210	–
Sewerby Yorks.	grave 10	C3 35.0	–	–	–	–
Sewerby Yorks.	grave 37	C2 29.8	conical	knife	–	–
Sewerby Yorks.	grave 45	E3 36.8	–	knife, shield	–	–
Shepperton I Middlesex	grave	J 18.2	–	–	Guildford Museum S.5958	*PSA.*, 2nd S. IV, 1868, 118.
Shepperton I Middlesex	grave	E3 f28.0f	–	–	Guildford Museum S.5959	*PSA.*, 2nd S. IV, 1868, 118.
Shepperton I Middlesex	grave	I1 f23.8	–	sword, shield	London Museum 0.2062	*PSA.*, 2nd S. IV, 1868, 118.
Sherrington Wilts.	grave A	H2 38.2	–	–	–	*Wilts.Arch.Magazine*, VI, 1860, 368, fig. 18.
Sherrington Wilts.	grave B	E2 31.8	–	knife, sword, shield	–	*Wilts.Arch.Magazine*, VI, 1860, 368, fig. 19.
Shipton Oxon.	?grave	L 23.9	–	–	Ashmolean Museum 1928 522	–
Shipton Oxon.	?grave	K1 f)22.3	–	–	Ashmolean Museum 1928 523	–
Shrewton Wilts.	–	C2 25.0	–	–	Salisbury Museum	*Wilts.Arch.Magazine*, XXXVIII, 1914, 321.
Shudy Camps Cambs.	grave 30	C2 28.5	–	knife	Cambridge Museum 36.848	*Cambridge Ant.Soc. Quarto Pubs.*, NS.V, 12, fig. 3.
Shudy Camps Cambs.	grave 36	C5 21.6	–	2 knives, seax	–	*Cambridge Ant.Soc. Quarto Pubs.*, NS.V, 14, fig. 3.
Shudy Camps Cambs.	grave 76	C2 22.0	–	(a female grave)	–	*Cambridge Ant.Soc. Quarto Pubs.*, NS.V, 23, fig. 11.
Sibertswold Kent	grave 23	F2 37.1	–	–	Liverpool Museum	–
Sibertswold Kent	grave 28	F2 40.0	–	knife	–	*Inventorium Sepulchrale*, 107, fig. 14.
Sibertswold Kent	grave 48	F2 c40.0	–	knife	–	*Inventorium Sepulchrale*, 110.
Sibertswold Kent	grave 58	F2 43.0f	–	seax, sword	–	*Inventorium Sepulchrale*, 111, fig. 14.
Sibertswold Kent	grave 59	C2 33.0	–	knife	–	*Faussett Papers*.
Sibertswold Kent	grave 64	F2 40.5	–	–	–	*Inventorium Sepulchrale*, 113.
Sibertswold Kent	grave 81	F2 c40.0	–	knife, shield	–	*Inventorium Sepulchrale*, 115.
Sibertswold Kent	grave 82	F2 45.5	–	knife, shield	–	*Inventorium Sepulchrale*, 115.
		F2 45.5	–		–	*Inventorium Sepulchrale*, 115.
Sibertswold Kent	grave 87	F2 c43.0	–	shield	–	*Faussett Papers*.
Sibertswold Kent	grave 91	E3	–	knife	–	*Faussett Papers*.
Sibertswold Kent	grave 92	C2 33.0	–	knife	–	*Faussett Papers*.
Sibertswold Kent	grave 97	F2 c40.0	–	shield	–	*Inventorium Sepulchrale*, 117.
Sibertswold Kent	grave 98	A2 23.5f	*	knife, sword	Liverpool Museum 6552	*Inventorium Sepulchrale*, 117, pl. xiv,4.
Sibertswold Kent	grave 99	F2	–	knife, shield	–	*Inventorium Sepulchrale*, 118.
Sibertswold Kent	grave 102	F2	*	knife, shield	–	*Inventorium Sepulchrale*, 118.
Sibertswold Kent	grave 105	C2 30.7	–	knife, shield	–	*Inventorium Sepulchrale*, 119.
Sibertswold Kent	grave 106	E3	–	–	–	*Inventorium Sepulchrale*, 119.

Provenance	Nature of find.	Type Length	Butt-ferrule	Associated weapons.	Museum Accession no.	Publication
Sibertswold Kent	grave 108	F2	*	knife, shield	-	*Inventorium Sepulchrale*, 119.
Sibertswold Kent	grave 109	F2	-	knife, shield	-	*Inventorium Sepulchrale*, 119.
Sibertswold Kent	grave 110	F2	-	knife	-	*Faussett Papers*.
Sibertswold Kent	grave 111	F2	-	knife, shield	-	*Inventorium Sepulchrale*, 120.
Sibertswold Kent	grave 112	E3	-	knife, shield	-	*Inventorium Sepulchrale*, 120.
Sibertswold Kent	grave 113	F2	conical	knife	-	*Inventorium Sepulchrale*, 120.
Sibertswold Kent	grave 115	E3 60.5	-	knife, shield	-	*Inventorium Sepulchrale*, 120, pl.xiv.
Sibertswold Kent	grave 117	F2	-	knife, seax, shield	-	*Inventorium Sepulchrale*, 120.
Sibertswold Kent	grave 123	E3	*	knife	-	*Inventorium Sepulchrale*, 122.
Sibertswold Kent	grave 126	E3	-	shield	-	*Inventorium Sepulchrale*, 122.
Sibertswold Kent	grave 128	F1 14.0	-	knife	-	*Faussett Papers*.
Sibertswold Kent	grave 132	E3	-	knife, shield	-	*Inventorium Sepulchrale*, 123.
Sibertswold Kent	grave 140	F2	-	2 knives, sword	-	*Inventorium Sepulchrale*, 124.
Sibertswold Kent	grave 150	F2	-	-	-	*Inventorium Sepulchrale*, 124.
Sibertswold Kent	grave 157	F2	-	knife	-	*Inventorium Sepulchrale*, 126.
Sibertswold Kent	grave 176	F2	cylindrical	seax	-	*Inventorium Sepulchrale*, 132.
Sibertswold/Barfreston, Kent	grave 33	E3	conical	knife	-	*Faussett Papers*.
Sileby Leics.	?grave	C2 17.9f	-	-	Leicester Museum 335 1958	-
Skyrethorne Yorks.	-	B1 27.1	-	-	Skipton Museum	-
Sleaford Lincs.	grave 119	C2 35.5f	-	-	British Museum 83 4-1 586	*Archaeologia*, L, 1887, 396, pl. xxv,7.
Sleaford Lincs.	grave 152	E1	-	shield	-	*Archaeologia*, L, 1887, 399.
Sleaford Lincs.	grave	C4 48.3	-	-	British Museum 83 4-1 552	-
Sleaford Lincs.	grave	H3 42.9	-	-	British Museum 83 4-1 553	-
Sleaford Lincs.	grave	H3 f)40.0	-	-	British Museum 83 4-1 554	-
Sleaford Lincs.	grave	H3 33.6(f	-	-	British Museum 83 4-1 555	-
Sleaford Lincs.	grave	H3 35.9	-	-	British Museum 83 4-1 556	-
Sleaford Lincs.	grave	H3 f)33.9	-	-	British Museum 83 4-1 557	-
Sleaford Lincs.	grave	G1 34.2	-	-	British Museum 83 4-1 558	*Spearheads*, fig. 35a.
Sleaford Lincs.	grave	H3 f)32.1	-	-	British Museum 83 4-1 559	-
Sleaford Lincs.	grave	H2 30.9	-	-	British Museum 83 4-1 560	-
Sleaford Lincs.	grave	H2 31.0	-	-	British Museum 83 4-1 561	-
Sleaford Lincs.	grave	H3 31.3	-	-	British Museum 83 4-1 562	-
Sleaford Lincs.	grave	H2 29.1	-	-	British Museum 83 4-1 563	-

Provenance	Nature of find.	Type Length	Butt-ferrule	Associated weapons.	Museum Accession no.	Publication
Sleaford Lincs.	grave	H2 28.9	-	-	British Museum 83 4-1 564	-
Sleaford Lincs.	grave	F2 f26.4	-	-	British Museum 83 4-1 565	-
Sleaford Lincs.	grave	C2 23.9	-	-	British Museum 83 4-1 566	-
Sleaford Lincs.	grave	H2 f)26.7	-	-	British Museum 83 4-1 567	-
Sleaford Lincs.	grave	H2 f20.7f	-	-	British Museum 83 4-1 568	-
Sleaford Lincs.	grave	H2 26.9	-	-	British Museum 83 4-1 569	-
Sleaford Lincs.	grave	H2 f21.0f	-	-	British Museum 83 4-1 570	-
Sleaford Lincs.	grave	E1 19.7(f	-	-	British Museum 83 4-1 571	-
Sleaford Lincs.	grave	H2 f)25.0	-	-	British Museum 83 4-1 572	-
Sleaford Lincs.	grave	H2 f)20.1f	-	-	British Museum 83 4-1 573	-
Sleaford Lincs.	grave	H2 23.0	-	-	British Museum 83 4-1 574	-
Sleaford Lincs.	grave	E2 21.8	-	-	British Museum 83 4-1 575	-
Sleaford Lincs.	grave	E4 f21.6f	-	-	British Museum 83 4-1 576	-
Sleaford Lincs.	grave	H1 f)17.8(f	-	-	British Museum 83 4-1 577	-
Sleaford Lincs.	grave	F1 18.0	-	-	British Museum 83 4-1 578	-
Sleaford Lincs.	grave	E1 f)16.9	-	-	British Museum 83 4-1 579	-
Sleaford Lincs.	grave	E1 16.8	-	-	British Museum 83 4-1 580	-
Sleaford Lincs.	grave	E2 f16.2	-	-	British Museum 83 4-1 581	-
Sleaford Lincs.	grave	F1 15.8	-	-	British Museum 83 4-1 582	-
Sleaford Lincs.	grave	H1 f)15.8	-	-	British Museum 83 4-1 583	-
Sleaford Lincs.	grave	H1 f)14.5	-	-	British Museum 83 4-1 584	-
Sleaford Lincs.	grave	E1 12.0	-	-	British Museum 83 4-1 585	-
Sleaford Lincs.	grave	C4 f40.2f	-	-	British Museum 83 4-1 587	-
Sleaford Lincs.	grave	G2 f)38.6f	-	-	British Museum 83 4-1 588	-
Sleaford Lincs.	grave	H2 f21.2	-	-	British Museum 83 4-1 589	-
Sleaford Lincs.	grave	E3 f)27.8f	-	-	British Museum 83 4-1 590	-
Sleaford Lincs.	grave	H2 f)24.9f	-	-	British Museum 83 4-1 591	-
Sleaford Lincs.	grave	E1 17.8	-	-	British Museum 83 4-1 592	-
Sleaford Lincs.	grave	H1 f)17.7	-	-	British Museum 83 4-1 593	-
Sleaford Lincs.	grave	E1 f8.0f	-	-	British Museum 83 4-1 598	-
Sleaford Lincs.	grave	L f24.0	-	-	Lincoln Museum 816-23.09	-
Sleaford Lincs.	grave	C2 f)11.1f	-	-	Lincoln Museum 816-23.09	- .
Sleaford Lincs.	grave	C2 f)24.6f	-	-	Lincoln Museum 816-23.09	-

Provenance	Nature of find.	Type Length	Butt-ferrule	Associated weapons.	Museum Accession no.	Publication
Sleaford Lincs.	grave	H2 28.7	-	-	Lincoln Museum 816-23.09	-
Sleaford Lincs.	grave	C3 36.8	-	-	Lincoln Museum 816-23.09	-
Sleaford Lincs.	grave	H3 37.8	-	-	Lincoln Museum 816-23.09	-
Sleaford Lincs.	grave	E3 f)38.5f	-	-	Lincoln Museum 816-23.09	-
Sleaford Lincs.	grave	E3 f)51.1	-	-	Lincoln Museum 816-23.09	-
Sleaford Lincs.	grave	E3 f48.2f	-	-	Lincoln Museum 816-23.09	-
Sleaford Lincs.	grave	E3 40.9f	-	-	Lincoln Museum 816-23.09	-
Sleaford Lincs.	grave	E4 f31.3f	-	-	Lincoln Museum 816-23.09	-
Sleaford Lincs.	grave	E4 f37.3	-	-	Lincoln Museum 816-23.09	-
Snells Corner Hants.	grave 12	E2 f)28.9	-	knife	Portsmouth Museum 111.56	Proc.Hants.Field Club, XIX, 1957, 128, fig.11,1.
Snells Corner Hants.	grave 14	C4 47.2	-	shield	Portsmouth Museum 115.56	Proc.Hants.Field Club, XIX, 1957, 128, fig.12,1.
Snells Corner Hants.	grave 20	C2 32.9	conical 5.6	knife, shield	Portsmouth Museum 121.56	Proc.Hants.Field Club, XIX, 1957, 131m fig.13,1-2.
Snells Corner Hants.	grave 25	C2 24.5	-	-	Portsmouth Museum 128.56	Proc.Hants.Field Club, XIX, 1957, 132.
Snells Corner Hants.	grave 26	C2 f)20.5	-	knife	Portsmouth Museum 124.56	Proc.Hants.Field Club, XIX, 1957, 132, fig.14,1.
Soham B Cambs.	?grave	H2 27.7	-	-	British Museum 76 2-12 57	-
Soham B Cambs.	?grave	F2 22.7	-	-	British Museum 76 2-12 58	-
Soham Cambs.	?grave	B2 26.4	-	-	Cambridge Museum 34.968	-
Soham Cambs.	?grave	C2 27.5	-	-	Cambridge Museum 34.969	-
Sonning Berks.	River Thames	I2 26.5	-	-	Reading Museum 1.56	Spearheads, fig. 47a.
Sonning Berks.	River Thames	I2 18.8	-	-	Reading Museum	Berks.Arch.Journal, LIX, 1960, 119, fig. 11.
South Shields Durham	Roman Fort	A1 29.9(f	-	-	Newcastle Museum	Arch.Aeliana, 2nd S. X, 1885, 271.
Southwark London	-	E2 26.6	-	-	Guildhall Museum, London 4060	-
Spettisbury Dorset	-	E2 24.9	-	-	British Museum 62 6-27 6	-
Spettisbury Dorset	-	E1 12.8	-	-	British Museum 62 6-27 7	-
pet isbury Dorset	-	C1 10.0	-	-	British Museum 62 6-27 8	-
Spettisbury Dorset	-	B1 24.9	-	-	British Museum 62 6-27 9	Spearheads, fig. 6d.
Spittlegate Lincs.	grave	H2 27.3	-	-	Grantham Museum AS.9	-
Spittlegate Lincs.	grave	E2 f)21.8f	-	-	Grantham Museum AS.12	-
Spittlegate Lincs.	grave	C3 28.8	-	-	Grantham Museum AS.13	-
Spittlegate Lincs.	grave	E2 f)22.6	-	-	Grantham Museum AS.14	Spearheads, fig. 25b.
Spittlegate Lincs.	grave	E4 f)23.5(f	-	-	Grantham Museum AS.23	-
Spittlegate Lincs.	grave	C3 f)24.8f	-	-	Grantham Museum AS.26	-
Staines Middlesex	River Thames	C3 24.5	-	-	British Museum 1960 12-2 2	-

Provenance	Nature of find.	Type Length	Butt-ferrule	Associated weapons.	Museum Accession no.	Publication
Staines Middlesex	River Thames	C1 16.1	-	-	Reading Museum 11.56	Berks.Arch.Journal, LVI, 1958, 56.
Stanlake Oxon.	grave	E4 f)28.0	-	2 knives	Ashmolean Museum 1921 1118	Berks.Bucks.& Oxon. Arch.J., IV, 1898, 39.
Stanground Hunts.	grave	H3 55.2	-	-	Peterborough Museum L.567	-
Stanton Harcourt I, Oxon.	grave 15	C1 11.7	-	knife	Ashmolean Museum 1940 194	Oxoniensia, X, 1945, 38, fig. 10.
Stapenhill Staffs.	grave 21	E1 12.8	-	shield	-	Trans.Burton Arch.Soc., I, 1889, 166, pl.viii,21.
Stapenhill Staffs.	grave	F1 15.0	-	-	-	Trans.Burton Arch.Soc., I, 1889, 165.
Stapenhill Staffs.	grave	C2 28.0	-	-	-	Trans.Burton Arch.Soc., I, 1889, 165.
Stapenhill Staffs.	grave	F3 f36.6f	-	-	Burton-on-Trent Museum	-
Stapenhill Staffs.	grave	H3 29.7f	-	-	Burton-on-Trent Museum	-
Stapenhill Staffs.	grave	C3 26.7f	-	-	Burton-on-Trent Museum	-
Stapleford Park Leics.	grave	E4 f28.5(f	-	-	Leicester Museum I.IL 1946	-
Stapleford Park Leics.	grave	E1 f8.7f	-	-	Leicester Museum I.IL 1946	-
Stapleford Park Leics.	grave	E4 f14.2f	-	-	Leicester Museum 5 1947	-
Stapleford Park Leics.	grave	H2 20.6	-	-	Leicester Museum 5 1947	-
Stapleford Park Leics.	grave	L 27.7	-	-	Leicester Museum 5 1947	-
Staxton Yorks.	grave 83	H2 28.9	-	-	Hull Museum	The Naturalist, 1938, 110, pl.
Staxton Yorks.	grave 84	H2 f22.0	-	-	Hull Museum	The Naturalist, 1938, 110, pl.
Staxton Yorks.	grave 85	D1 14.8	-	-	Hull Museum	The Naturalist, 1938, 110, pl.
Staxton Yorks.	grave	C3 f)30.9f	-	-	Scarborough Museum 349.56	-
Steep Lowe Staffs.	grave	C2 27.2	-	knife, smaller spear	Sheffield Museum J.93.1130	Antiquities Derbyshire, 176-7, fig.
Stockholm Farm Berks.	grave	E3 f46.9f	-	-	Swindon Museum	-
Stockholm Farm Berks.	grave	H3 f)27.8f	-	-	Swindon Museum	-
Stourton Wilts.	grave	H1 17.5	-	knife, shield	Devizes Museum 115	The Stourhead Collection, 80.
Stowting Kent	grave 1	C2 24.2	-	-	-	JBAA., XXXIX, 1883, 84, fig.
Stowting Kent	grave 2	E4 f)38.0	-	-	-	JBAA., XXXIX, 1883, 84, fig.
Stowting Kent	grave 3	D1 27.9(f	-	-	-	JBAA., XXXIX, 1883, 84, fig.
Stratford Warwicks.	grave 2	F2 f16.3f	-	shield	Stratford Museum	-
Stratford Warwicks.	grave 6	C2 20.2f	-	knife, shield	Stratford Museum	-
Stratford Warwicks.	grave 17	E1 15.3	conical 6.4	-	Stratford Museum	Spearheads, fig. 31a.
Stratford Warwicks.	grave 30	H3 37.9	-	knife, shield	Stratford Museum	-
		J f20.7	-		Stratford Museum	-
Stratford Warwicks.	grave 31	H3 34.1f	conical 8.4	-	Stratford Museum	- .
Stratford Warwicks.	grave 34	H3 f27.5	conical 5.0	-	Stratford Museum	-

Provenance	Nature of find.	Type Length	Butt-ferrule	Associated weapons.	Museum Accession no.	Publication
Stratford Warwicks.	grave 39	H3 30.7	-	shield	Stratford Museum	-
		C2 f31.9	-		Stratford Museum	-
Stratford Warwicks.	grave 45	H3 40.2	-	knife, shield	Stratford Museum	-
Stratford Warwicks.	grave 56	E1 13.5	-	knife	Stratford Museum	-
Stratford Warwicks.	grave 58	D3 31.0f	-	-	Stratford Museum	*Spearheads*, fig. 21a.
Stratford Warwicks.	grave 67	E1 16.4	-	-	Stratford Museum	-
Stratford Warwicks.	grave 69	C2 22.6	-	-	Stratford Museum	-
Stratford Warwicks.	grave 73	H2 24.5	-	knife	Stratford Museum	-
		H2 20.3	-		Stratford Museum	-
Stratford Warwicks.	grave 74	C2 f24.5f	-	knife	Stratford Museum	-
Stratford Warwicks.	grave 84	E1 19.2	-	-	Stratford Museum	-
Stratford Warwicks.	grave 92	C4 43.3	-	-	Stratford Museum	-
Stratford Warwicks.	grave 188	H1 19.1	-	-	Stratford Museum	-
Stratford Warwicks.	grave	H2 f)23.2	-	-	Stratford Museum	-
Stratford Warwicks.	grave	G1 f23.4	-	-	Stratford Museum	-
Stratford Warwicks.	grave	G1 f28.0	-	-	Stratford Museum	-
Stratford Warwicks.	grave	E1 19.3	-	-	Stratford Museum	-
Stratford Warwicks.	grave	E1 19.5	-	-	Stratford Museum	-
Stratford Warwicks.	grave	H2 22.7	-	-	Stratford Museum	-
Stratford Warwicks.	grave	C2 f23.5	-	-	Stratford Museum	-
Stratford Warwicks.	grave	G1 f25.1f	-	-	Stratford Museum	-
Stratford Warwicks.	grave	C3 f23.4	-	-	Stratford Museum	-
Stratford Warwicks.	grave	C1 f13.9	-	-	Stratford Museum	-
Stratford Warwicks.	grave	E1 f11.6f	-	-	Stratford Museum	-
Street Ashton Warwicks.	?grave	H2 23.5	-	-	Warwick Museum	*Arts in Early England*, III, 186, pl. xx,3.
Stretton-on-Fosse Warwicks.	grave 2	C1 15.0	-	knife	Warwick Museum	-
Stretton-on-Fosse Warwicks.	grave 3	H1 f)11.9(f	-	arrow	Warwick Museum	-
Stretton-on-Fosse Warwicks.	grave 4	H3 39.6	-	shield	Warwick Museum	*Spearheads*, 207.
Stretton-on-Fosse Warwicks.	grave 8	C1 16.2	-	knife	Warwick Museum	-
Stretton-on-Fosse Warwicks.	grave 9	H2 24.0	-	shield	Warwick Museum	-
Stretton-on-Fosse Warwicks.	grave 10	C1 12.6	-	shield	Warwick Museum	-
		H3 35.7	-		Warwick Museum	-
Stretton-on-Fosse Warwicks.	grave 11	E1 15.4	-	knife, shield	Warwick Museum	-

Provenance	Nature of find.	Type Length	Butt-ferrule	Associated weapons.	Museum Accession no.	Publication
Stretton-on-Fosse Warwicks.	grave 12	E1 22.6	-	-	Warwick Museum	-
Stretton-on-Fosse Warwicks.	grave 17	H1 16.2	-	-	Warwick Museum	-
Stretton-on-Fosse Warwicks.	grave 20	E1 15.6	-	-	Warwick Museum	-
Stretton-on-Fosse Warwicks.	grave 30	H1 18.9	-	-	Warwick Museum	-
Stretton-on-Fosse Warwicks.	grave 38	L f)12.4f	-	knife, shield	Warwick Museum	-
Stretton-on-Fosse Warwicks.	grave 50	H1 22.2	-	shield	Warwick Museum	-
Strood I Kent	grave 3	H2 26.6	-	knife, sword, shield	-	*Collectanea Antiqua*, II, 158-9, pl.xxxvi.
Strood II Kent	grave	A2 44.1f	cylindrical 3.8	knife, sword, shield	British Museum 94 8-3 81	*Collectanea Antiqua*, V, 129-35, pl.xi.
		F2 23.6	-		British Museum 94 8-3 82	*Collectanea Antiqua*, V, 129-35, pl.xi.
Summertown Oxon.	grave	K1 32.5	-	shield	Ashmolean Museum 1966 575	-
Surbiton Surrey	River Thames	I2 28.3	-	-	Reading Museum	-
Surley Hall Point, Berks.	River Thames	H2 25.2	-	-	Reading Museum 292.47	-
Sutton Hoo Suffolk	ship-burial	A2 76.0	conical 5.6	seax, sword, axe-hammer, shield, byrnie, helmet, another spear	British Museum 1939 10-10 98	*Antiqu.Journal*, XX, 1940, 163, 195, pl.xix.
		A2 68.0	conical 5.4		British Museum 1939 10-10 99	*Antiqu.Journal*, XX, 1940, 163, 195, pl.xix.
		A2 f62.0	conical 4.8f		British Museum 1939 10-10 100	*Antiqu.Journal*, XX, 1940, 163, 195, pl.xix.
		G2 38.7f	-		British Museum 1939 10-10 101	*Antiqu.Journal*, XX, 1940, 163, 195, pl.xix.
		D2 39.8f	-		British Museum 1939 10-10 102	*Antiqu.Journal*, XX, 1940, 163, 195, pl.xix.
		C2 32.2	-		British Museum 1939 10-10 103	*Antiqu.Journal*, XX, 1940, 163, 195, pl.xix.
		import 44.2	-		British Museum 1939 10-10 104	*Antiqu.Journal*, XX, 1940, 163, 195, pl.xix.
Sutton Scotney Hants.	grave	F2 37.0	-	-	Winchester Museum	-
Swaffham Norfolk	grave	H2 25.8	-	-	Norwich Museum	-
Swaffham Norfolk	grave	H3 29.6f	-	-	Norwich Museum	-
Swallowcliffe Down, Wilts.	grave	C2 18.5f	-	-	Avebury Museum	*Spearheads*, 161.
Sweethope Northumberland	-	E2 25.5	-	-	British Museum 79 12-9 2079	-
Swindon (Evelyn St), Wilts.	grave	C2 16.6	-	knife	Swindon Museum	*Wilts.Arch.Magazine*, XLVI, 1934, 156.
Syonsby Leics.	-	B1 21.0f	-	-	Leicester Museum 70 1918	-
Taplow Bucks.	grave	A2 f51.8f	-	knife, sword, 2 shields, 2 other spears	British Museum 83 12-14 73,74	*JBAA.*, XL, 1884, 64, 66, fig. 2.
Thames Oxon.	river-find	C3 22.7f	-	-	Ashmolean Museum	-
Thames Oxon.	river-find	E4 38.6	-	-	Ashmolean Museum	-
Thames Oxon.	river-find	E4 36.7	-	-	Ashmolean Museum	-
Thames	river-find	D3 33.3	-	-	British Museum 68 9-4 3	-
Thames	river-find	B1 37.6	-	-	British Museum 68 9-4 13	*Spearheads*, fig. 6c.
Thames	river-find	E3 30.6f	-	-	British Museum 88 7-19 46	-

Provenance	Nature of find.	Type Length	Butt-ferrule	Associated weapons.	Museum Accession no.	Publication
Thames	river-find	E3 f)35.5	-	-	British Museum 88 7-19 48	-
Thames	river-find	C2 29.1	-	-	British Museum 88 7-19 49	-
Thames	river-find	F2 21.9f	-	-	British Museum 88 7-19 51	-
Thames	river-find	E2 f)18.2f	-	-	British Museum 88 7-19 52	-
Thames	river-find	F2 26.6	-	-	British Museum 88 7-19 53	-
Thames	river-find	F2 24.1	-	-	British Museum 88 7-19 54	-
Thames	river-find	F1 f16.6f	-	-	British Museum 88 7-19 55	-
Thames	river-find	B1 30.3	-	-	British Museum 88 7-19 60	-
Thames	river-find	E3 f31.5f	-	-	British Museum	-
Thames	river-find	E2 f20.9f	-	-	Cuming, Museum, Southwark 308	
Thames	river-find	C2 23.7	-	-	London Museum A.3821	
Thames	river-find	D3 16.9	-	-	London Museum A.3822	
Thames Berks.	river-find	D2 39.2	-	-	Reading Museum 254.61	-
Thames Essex	river-find	E3 f37.2f	-	-	Tilbury Museum 133	-
Thames Hurley Berks.	River Thames	D2 f23.2f	-	-	Reading Museum 277.47	-
Thetford I Norfolk	grave	C3 48.2	-	knife, shield	Thetford Museum	*Norfolk Archaeology*, XXVII, 1939, 240, pl.xiv.
Thetford II Norfolk	grave	J f28.8	-	-	Kings Lynn Museum	-
Thorpe Malsor Northants.	grave	H2 20.6f	-	shield	Kettering Museum 1961 43.5	-
Thorpe Malsor Northants.	grave	H2 23.1f	-	shield	Kettering Museum 1961 43.6	
Threckingham Lincs.	-	C2 f)24.0	-	-	Lincoln Museum 51.57	*Proc.Lincs.A.&.A.Soc.*, VII, 1958, 110.
Thurnham Kent	grave	G1 f)16.9f	-	-	-	*Antiqu.Journal*, XX, 1940, 381-2, fig.2.
Thurnham Kent	grave	D3 27.8	-	-	-	*Antiqu.Journal*, XX, 1940, 381-2, fig.2.
Tilton-on-the-Hill, Leics.	surface-find	E3 f30.6	-	-	Leicester Museum 249 1959	-
Titterstone Clee, Shrops.	surface-find	C2 f)23.7	-	-	British Museum 1933 5-8 1	*Antiqu.Journal*, XIV, 1934, 32, fig.2.
Toddington I Beds.	grave	K2 f)28.1	-	knife, shield	Luton Museum 2.356.40	*PSA.*, 2nd S. X, 1883-5, 36.
Tollerton Notts.	-	E3 37.9f	-	-	York Museum 1960	-
Tottenhill Norfolk	?grave	C3 f25.2f	-	-	Kings Lynn Museum	*PPSEA.*, I, 1911, 118.
Totternhoe Beds.	grave 11	E3 f)46.5(f	-	knife	Luton Museum 13.120.58	*Beds.Arch.Journal*, I, 1962, 29, fig.
Trumpington Cambs.	-	C3 f)26.5f	-	-	Cambridge Museum	-
Uley Glos.	grave	F2 36.5	-	-	Stroud Museum	-
Upper Swell II Glos.	grave	C1 21.9	-	knife	Bristol Museum	*Trans.Bristol & Glos.A.S.*, LXXXVIII, 1964, 13, fig.1q.
Upper Upham Wilts.	?grave	E1 24.8	-	-	Ashmolean Museum 1955 354c	-
Vincent Knoll Derbs.	grave	E1 f13.4	-	-	Sheffield Museum J.93.1165	*Ten Years' Digging*, 49.

Provenance	Nature of find	Type Length	Butt-ferrule	Associated weapons.	Museum Accession no.	Publication
Wallingford Berks.	grave 22	L f)26.3	-	knife, shield	Ashmolean Museum 1939 456	-
Wandsworth London	River Thames	D3 28.5	-	-	London Museum A.5605	London & the Saxons, 174, fig. 41.
Wandsworth London	River Thames	E4 46.1	-	-	London Museum A.15458	London & the Saxons, 173, pl.12,2.
Wandsworth London	River Thames	I2 31.7	-	-	London Museum A.15461	London & the Saxons, 168, pl.x,1.
Warren Hill Suffolk	grave	I2 31.9	-	knife, 2 shields	Pitt-Rivers Museum, Farnham	-
Warren Hill Suffolk	-	C3 38.2	-	-	Toronto Museum 927.66.19	-
Welbeck Hill Lincs.	grave 11	C2 32.9	-	knife	-	-
Welbeck Hill Lincs.	grave 12	H3 50.2	conical 8.5	knife	-	Spearheads, 207, fig.82e.
Welbeck Hill Lincs.	grave 17	H3 33.7	-	knife, shield	-	-
Welbeck Hill Lincs.	grave 29	C4 35.6	-	knife	-	-
Welbeck Hill Lincs.	grave 60	H2 28.0	-	knife	-	Spearheads, 203.
Welbeck Hill Lincs.	grave 63	C1 18.0	-	knife, shield	-	-
Wereham Norfolk	-	H2 f)27.4	-	-	Kings Lynn Museum	-
West Ham Hants.	grave	C4 25.3f	-	knife	British Museum 1908 2-17 3	Acta Archaeologia, XVI, 1945, 15, fig.12.
West Ham Hants.	grave	C2 f)18.8	-	knife	British Museum 1908 2-17 4	Acta Archaeologia, XVI, 1945, 15, fig.11.
West Chisenbury Wilts.	grave	C2 28.8	-	-	Devizes Museum 121	Devizes Museum Catalogue, II, 248.
West Lodge Dorset	grave	E2 f18.9f	-	-	British Museum 92 9-1 1732	-
West Stow Heath Suffolk	grave	E1 f)17.1	-	-	Bury St Edmunds Museum K.48	Proc.Bury & W.Suffolk Arch.Inst., I, 1853, 328.
West Stow Heath Suffolk	grave	E1 21.6(f	-	-	Bury St Edmunds Museum K.48	Proc.Bury & W.Suffolk Arch.Inst., I, 1853, 328.
West Stow Heath Suffolk	grave	H2 f)22.9(f	-	-	Bury St Edmunds Museum K.48	Proc.Bury & W.Suffolk Arch.Inst., I, 1853, 328.
West Stow Heath Suffolk	grave	D1 25.1	-	-	Bury St Edmunds Museum K.71	-
West Stow Heath Suffolk	grave	J 29.2	-	-	Bury St Edmunds Museum K.72	-
Wetton Staffs.	grave	C3 f)26.0f	-	knife	Sheffield Museum J.93.1128	Ten Years' Digging, 194.
Weybridge Surrey	River Wey	D3 26.5	-	-	-	Surrey Arch.Collections, XXV, 1912, 133, pl.ii,6.
Wheatley Oxon.	grave 5	D2 25.5	-	-	Ashmolean Museum 1883 2b	PSA., 2nd S. XX X, 1916, 50, fig. 1d.
Wheatley Oxon.	grave 33b	C2 20.3	-	knife	-	PSA., 2nd S. XXIX, 1916, 56, fig. 1c.
Wheatley Oxon.	grave 33b	C2 21.5	-	knife	-	PSA., 2nd S. XXIX, 1916, 56, fig. 1e.
Wheatley Oxon.	grave	C3 f24.5	-	-	Ashmolean Museum	PSA., 2nd S. XXIX, 1916, 49, fig. 1b.
Wheatley Oxon.	grave	C4 31.5f	-	-	-	PSA., 2nd S. XXIX, 1916, 49.
Wheatley Oxon.	grave	H2 f15.6	-	-	-	PSA., 2nd S. XXIX, 1916, 49, fig. 1a.
Wheatley Oxon.	grave	C2 f)24.7	-	-	Ashmolean Museum 1883 21b	Proc.Birmingham Phil. Soc., IV, 1883-5, 186.
Wheatley Oxon.	grave	D1 22.6	-	-	Ashmolean Museum 1883 25	Proc.Birmingham Phil. Soc., IV, 1883-5, 186.
Wheatley Oxon.	grave	C2 21.3	-	-	Ashmolean Museum 1883 29b	Proc.Birmingham Phil. Soc., IV, 1883-5, 186.

Provenance	Nature of find.	Type Length	Butt-ferrule	Associated weapons.	Museum Accession no.	Publication
Wheatley Oxon.	grave	E4 36.8(f	-	-	Ashmolean Museum	-
Wichnor Staffs.	grave	D1 f40.2	-	-	-	Trans.Burton Arch.Soc., IV, 1899, 81.
Wichnor Staffs.	grave	H3 f30.9	-	-	-	Trans.Burton Arch.Soc., IV, 1899, 81.
Wichnor Staffs.	grave	H3 23.4f	-	-	-	Trans.Burton Arch.Soc., IV, 1899, 81.
Wichnor Staffs.	grave	C2 f41.2f	-	-	-	Trans.Burton Arch.Soc., IV, 1899, 81.
Wigber Low Derbs.	grave	D1 f16.5(f	-	-	British Museum 73 6-2 93	Spearheads, 171.
Wilfholme Yorks.	river-find	H2 26.3	-	-	Hull Museum	-
Wilsford Down Wilts.	-	C4 45.4f	-	-	Devizes Museum 534	-
Wiltshire	grave	C1 14.2f	-	another, larger spear	Barrow Museum C.21	-
Winchester I Hants.	grave	H2 24.2	-	shield	Winchester Museum	-
Winchester I Hants.	grave	C2 28.0	-	-	Winchester Museum	Spearheads, fig. 11d.
Winchester I Hants.	grave	H2 26.4	-	-	Winchester Museum	-
Winchester II Hants.	grave	H1 21.0	-	-	Winchester Museum	-
Winchester II Hants.	grave	E1 f17.8f	-	-	Winchester Museum	-
Windsor Berks.	River Thames	E1 f)21.1	-	-	Ashmolean Museum 1885 760	-
Windsor Berks.	River Thames	F2 29.5	-	-	Ashmolean Museum 1885 761	-
Windsor Berks.	River Thames	B2 23.5	-	-	Reading Museum 189.62	-
Winster Derbs.	grave 2	B1 61.0	-	knife	Sheffield Museum J.93.1178	JBAA., XIII, 1857, 227-8, fig.
Winterbourne Gunner, Wilts.	grave 1	C3 44.3	-	2 knives, shield	Salisbury Museum 56.61	Wilts.Arch.Magazine, LIX, 1964, 89, fig.5,Ia.
Winterbourne Gunner, Wilts.	grave 4	H2 23.9	-	shield	Salisbury Museum 56.61	Wilts.Arch.Magazine, LIX, 1964, 91, fig.5,IVa.
Winterslow Hut Wilts.	grave	C2 f24.4	-	shield	Ashmolean Museum	Wilts.Arch.Magazine, XLVIII, 1938, 176, pl.i.
Witherington Wilts.	grave	H2 27.2	conical 8.8	sword, shield	Salisbury Museum	Earthworks of the New Forest, 87.
Woking Park Farm Surrey	-	C1 10.0	-	-	Guildford Museum	Surrey Arch.Collections, XV, 1912, 140, pl.
Woodbridge Wilts.	grave A	E2 f)26.5	-	shield	Devizes Museum 62	Wilts.Arch.Magazine, XLVII, 1935, 265.
Woodford Wilts.	-	C2 f27.5	-	-	Salisbury Museum	Wilts.Arch.Magazine, XLVI, 1934, 174.
Woodingdean Sussex	grave 3	F2 f)22.9f	-	knife	Brighton Museum	Sussex Notes & Queries, XV, 1958, 69.
Woodyates Inn Wilts.	grave	C2 25.9	-	knife	Devizes Museum 119	Devizes Museum Catalogue, I, 62, fig.
Woolsthorpe Lincs.	grave	E2 f18.1f	-	-	Grantham Museum AS.15	-
Wootton Berks.	grave	C2 45.1	-	-	Ashmolean Museum 1960 1260	Spearheads, fig. 13c.
Worlaby Lincs.	grave 2	C2 18.2	-	knife	private collection	Spearheads, 163.
Worlaby Lincs.	grave 4	H2 19.2	-	knife, shield	Scunthorpe Museum	Spearheads, 203.
Worlebury Somerset	?grave	L f)19.3	-	-	Weston-super-Mare Museum	-
Worthy Park Hants.	grave 22	H2 26.5	conical 6.5	knife, shield	-	-

Provenance	Nature of find.	Type Length	Butt-ferrule	Associated weapons.	Museum Accession no.	Publication
Worthy Park Hants.	grave 24	E3 44.2	-	knife, shield	-	-
Worthy Park Hants.	grave 33	L f)25.1	-	knife, shield	-	-
Worthy Park Hants.	grave 44	H1 18.8	-	knife, shield	-	-
Worthy Park Hants.	grave 45	H1 21.6	conical 10.2	knife	-	-
Worthy Park Hants.	grave 46	H1 16.7	-	knife	-	-
Worthy Park Hants.	grave	J 24.3	-	seax, shield	-	*Spearheads*, 209, fig. 85a.
Worthy Park Hants.	grave 50	I1 31.6	conical 9.9	knife	-	*Spearheads*, 207, fig. 83b.
Worthy Park Hants.	grave 71	H1 f)16.9	-	knife	-	-
Worthy Park Hants.	grave 79	H3 41.8	-	-	-	-
Worthy Park Hants.	grave 81	I1 29.5	-	knife, shield	-	-
Worthy Park Hants.	grave 83	K1 34.3	-	knife	-	-
Worthy Park Hants.	grave 84	H1 20.1	-	knife	-	-
Worthy Park Hants.	grave 87	K1 24.2	-	knife, shield	-	-
Worthy Park Hants.	grave 94	E3 f)43.2	-	-	-	-
Worthy Park Hants.	grave 95	H2 f)24.0	-	knife, shield	-	-
Worthy Park Hants.	grave 97	C2 24.2	-	-	-	-
Wretton Norfolk	grave	E1 f)16.3f	-	knife, seax, shield	Norwich Museum 153.929	*Norfolk Archaeology*, XXVII, 1939, 233.
Wrotham II Kent	grave	E3 f)22.0f	-	knife, fourth spear	British Museum 1927 5-12 4	*Spearheads*, 181.
Wrotham II Kent	grave	E3 f18.8(f	-	knife, fourth spear	British Museum 1927 5-12 5	*Spearheads*, 181.
Wrotham II Kent	grave	E4 43.2	-	knife, fourth spear	British Museum 1927 5-12 8	*Spearheads*, 183, fig. 29c.
Wye I Kent	grave	C2 f19.5	-	-	British Museum 93 6-1 193	-
Yarnton Oxon.	grave	C2 f)27.0	-	knife, shield	Ashmolean Museum 1864 1444	G. Rolleston, *Scientific Papers*, II, 1884, 944.
Yarnton Oxon.	grave	H2 f22.2(f	-	-	Ashmolean Museum 1864 1444	G. Rolleston, *Scientific Papers*, II, 1884, 944.
York III Yorks.	grave	E2 f)19.2	-	-	Hull Museum	-
York III Yorks.	grave	C2 f)17.5	-	-	Hull Museum	-
York III Yorks.	grave	C3 21.7	-	-	Hull Museum	-
York III Yorks.	grave	H2 22.3(f	-	-	Hull Museum	-

www.ingramcontent.com/pod-product-compliance
Lightning Source LLC
Chambersburg PA
CBHW061547010526
44114CB00027B/2953